VEGAN DIET
YOUR COMPLETE GUIDE
TO A HEALTHY LIFE

About the Author

My name is Lilly Iaschelcic. Switching to a plant-based diet transformed my life entirely. I realized that the food we put in our bodies influences everything inside. As they say, "You are what you eat." Therefore, I became a supporter of Veganism.

Presently, I am pursuing a degree in osteopathic medicine and nutrition, which further signifies the incalculable benefits of a vegan diet on our health.

I have been an athletic individual for the past 15 years. Being a martial artist, black belt in taekwondo, plus a strict vegan, has helped me stand out in my athletic performance. I, myself, have recognized that strong athletic bodies are not only made in steakhouses. The previous school of thought that the vegan diet is intimidating has been proven false over the course of time.

This book focuses on clean vegan eating, which is super easy to manage and amazingly healthy. With the correct food resources and a little planning, switching to a whole-based vegan diet would be the best decision you ever made.

My publication further explains how plant-based plans can help you in your perfect eating venture and the idea of vegan fasting, which is a logical step for living a super active and conscious lifestyle. The book covers everything you need to know about veganism, ranging from the concept, history, and evolution to protein questions, vegan diet plans, the ultimate veganism guide, and the best vegan food cuisines and restaurants that I have discovered during my travel diaries.

I've been an athlete for the past 15 years and as a competitive taekwondo black belt, I can honestly say that veganism has helped to propel my winning performances.

So, no, athletic bodies are not only made in steakhouses. The old school claim that 'a vegan diet does not contain the essential nutrients for physical excellence' has been proven FALSE !!!

HOW AND WHY I STARTED DOING A VEGAN DIET AND WHY YOU SHOULD TOO

The real motivation behind my turning vegan was my love and affection for animals. All of it started from my childhood, as we had two cats and two dogs. I became inspired to be a vet doctor as many children around the age of five do. In addition to this, I remember when I used to visit my grandparents at their farm during the summer holidays, they had lots of animals and we became good friends. After high school, I went to a college of Veterinarian Medicine where I completed my first degree with honors. This is what made me change my nutritional preferences altogether; you don't want to hurt who you love, and with animals, it was the same kind of experience for me. I cared for them and nurtured them, so how could I slay them and eat them in the name of a good diet and better nutrition for myself??? It felt so mean…

Now, I have been a vegan for almost nine years and the results that I have witnessed all along are nothing less than superfluous. I recover/heal better and have been getting ever-improving athletic results as well. My achievements include receiving a silver medal at the

Russian National Championships with a personal best of 11.1 seconds in the 100-meter, placing third in a half marathon, and finishing as a UK Taekwondo champion gold medalist (2017-2019). There are many others to come.

At the moment, I am pursuing my second degree, which is in Osteopathic Medicine and Nutrition. I prepare healthy and nutritious diet diaries for my patients and it gives me immense joy to do so. They start seeing the healthy benefits of the plan in typically less than a 4-6 weeks. This is a big enough time window to allow the genes a chance to change and adapt to such a diet. I am also in favor of saving our environment, raising awareness regarding environmental impact, deforestation, pollution, and global warming.

Table of Contents

WHAT IS A VEGAN DIET?

We have seen that people are often confused with the actual meaning of a vegan lifestyle. There is something very perplexing in terms of the list of allowed and restricted items. The vegan lifestyle, having a wide perspective, isn't restricted to food only; instead, it is a restrictive approach that encourages abstaining from any products of animal origin. In this book, I have elaborated all the aspects of a vegan diet to make it clearer for beginners. Have a look to understand everything you need to know and start your vegan diet right away! Veganism became the top food trend when people realized the actual facts and benefits of eating a plant-based diet. Veganism was initially either a cause to eradicate animal cruelty or part of following religious teachings. Many ethical, environmental, and health reasons were also considered in this regard. In recent years, vegan diets gained more hype as it has been proven to be the healthiest lifestyle for weight maintenance and prevention of health conditions like cardiovascular disorders.

Starting a vegan diet might seem to be a tough decision, but it ultimately guarantees long-term positive health benefits. A strict vegan lifestyle demands a deep knowledge of each and every item a person consumes or utilizes in his daily routine. The availability of vegan products is also a challenge. Besides all these obstacles, a vegan lifestyle has utmost preference to sustaining a better healthy lifestyle. A plant-based diet avoids animal-derived foods such as dairy, eggs, meat, poultry, fish, and even animal byproducts such as honey. The diet promotes the consumption of fruits, vegetables, nuts, seeds, legumes, dairy, and protein alternatives of animal-derived foods.

There are various types of vegan diets that we'll discuss later, along with all the recommended vegan foods for a better understanding.

WHAT IS MEANT BY THE TERM "VEGANISM?"

Veganism is actually a term used to represent the way of leading a vegan lifestyle. It is a philosophy, and itself a lifestyle, that discourages all sorts of exploitation and inhumane behavior towards animals. The term veganism isn't only restrained to boycotting animal-derived foods, but it is also committed to warding off animal testing and clothing made
from animal skins. Veganism elevates the need for animal-free food alternatives to maintain the ecosystem.
One belief of veganism is that killing innocent creatures for the sake of our personal needs isn't virtuous. They say that it isn't acceptable for them that the useless animals or the ones that are expensive to keep alive are brutally killed.

HISTORY OF VEGANISM

Veganism has many true origins of eradication of all sorts of exploitations and conserving the socio-economic system. In ancient times, some prominent historical figures laid down the foundation of veganism as the prevention of animal cruelty. The vegan diet does not have a specific point of origination. The idea of veganism was just a thought in the beginning;
later, it evolved as a concept and was termed as 'veganism.' The concept of veganism is regarded to Pythagoras, Porphyry,

Theophrastus, Benjamin Franklin, Hinduism, and Christianity.

Pythagoras

Pythagoras, an ancient Greek Philosopher, was famous for the creation of his mathematical theorem of hypotenuse of a right angle. Going back to 500 BCE, Pythagoras became the father of veganism when he introduced a meatless diet. The Pythagoras concept was considered a philosophical idea of morality to not kill living creatures, stop bloodshed in sacrificing animals, and eating meatless food. Pythagoras is so closely related to this concept that, until the word "vegetarianism" was recognized, these diets were known as "Pythagorean."

The outlook of Pythagoras' perspectives was that the hunger and cravings of the wicked human stomach can never be fulfilled with the blood and flesh of innocent animals. Not only Pythagoras, but also his followers, adapted the vegan diet for many reasons. Pythagoras believed in the reincarnation of souls and they claimed that without the exception of animals, all livings beings have souls and they cannot be slaughtered for our interests. They decided to live a green life with lots of vegetables, along with some bread and honey.

Regardless of how people admired this concept, many of them criticized him and he often faced ostracism. The disbelievers of this concept boycotted the Pythagoras because, at the time in the Greek Society, people used to celebrate food festivals that were primarily based on animal flesh. Pythagoras considered veganism as an act of kindness and tenderness towards the lower animals and a practice of philanthropy. Following this, Pythagoras and his disciples lead a simple life of bread, honey, and vegetables and considered it more ethical and even healthier than a meat-based diet. Later on, this concept of Pythagoras gained the acceptance of many religious figures and was also scientifically complimented. Mahatma Gandhi, George Bernard Shaw, and Bronson Alcott are amongst the early vegetarians.

Porphyry

Back to 250 CE, Porphyry was another Greek Philosopher in favor of a vegan diet. Porphyry was a prolific author and wrote about a diverse number of topics. He was actually a follower of Pythagoras and while supporting the vegan lifestyle Porphyry wrote a letter 'On Abstinence from Animal Food.' His letter had beautiful and logical reasons for the people to persue a vegan lifestyle. In the letter, he claimed that one should be clear about the fact that it is unjust to brutally kill the innocent and should neither utilize any of their derived products such as honey, wool, or milk.

Porphyry was of the view that necessities of life are few and can be gained without causing any harm or injury to innocent creatures. He illustrated this fact in the way that it is as similar as you tear the garments of an injured person amongst you. He said that the milk produced by the animals is not for us; instead, it is for their young ones.

In addition, honey produced by the bee is food for themselves and not to entertain us. He further elucidated his points by explaining the point of radical injustice, that we consume fruits but do not cut the trunks. Similarly, leguminous vegetables and other crops are consumed once they are fallen dead on the earth.

On the contrary, animals need to be slaughtered for food and dead animal corpse flesh is not eaten, so there is in these things a radical injustice. His critics contended that justice can only be done within the same species, and according to this, humans cannot do irrational things with animals. Porphyry argued that justice is extended to every living creature and every being that has a soul and participates in sense and memory is rational. His arguments were authentic and he convinced many others through his responses towards anti-vegan claims.

Watson's Vegan Society

At the age of 14, a pig slaughtered at his uncle's farm terrified Donald Watson. The screaming pig that was being murdered made him quit eating meat, and dairy as well. The barbarous act left a deep impression on the young boy's personality.

In 1944, as an adult, Donald Watson held a meeting with five other vegetarians that felt a need to properly give a specific name to their belief. Various suggestions were considered, such as dairyban, vitan, and benevore. Despite all the contrary views and oppositions, these six people pioneered the idea. Finally, after several discussions with his fiancé, they introduced the term "vegan" which was previously just a thought for everyone. He founded a 'Vegan Society' that started with only 25 members. It has now advanced for the guidance of various perspectives of veganism. It became registered in August 1964 and later on became a delimited liability company in December 1979. His first writing about veganism was published as *The Vegan News* in which he boldly presented his critical thinking. The *Vegan News* brought attention towards animal food believing that it was the extract of cruelty and brutality.

Watson proved that a change or revolution always came with human determination and his whole life was spent as an advocate for animal rights. As the foundation of vegan society was laid down in November, Watson suggested to celebrate the world's Vegan day in the month of November, so November 1 is officially recognized as "World Vegan Day."

In one of his interviews mentioning The Vegan Society, he boasted that the Genie is now out of the bottle, and no one can stop it. This society evolved in many ways with lots of amendments in their perspectives and objectives and is now considered as a refined group. The vegan society has made tremendous progress!

RELATIONSHIP BETWEEN VEGANISM AND RELIGION

Various religions encourage the veganism concept due to animal exploitation. They also practice animal product fasting during a certain time of the year. Christianity, Jainism, Buddhism, and Hinduism are prominent in this regard.

Hinduism
Hindu manuscripts and religious writings have strongly supported the ethical and spiritual benefits of a vegan diet. Hindus contemplate the concept of veganism as a religious practice and do not eat meat on particular days. Veganism is deeply rooted in Hindu customs and has especially adapted the Brahmin caste (highest caste of Hindus; the priests) by whom a vegan diet is considered on top of pious dietary regimes.

Hindus following vegan dietary patterns strictly consider the Dharmic Law and the Karmic results which states that no creation of God is to be harmed and that causing injury or inflicting suffering to any creature will come your way in the future, causing equal damage and sufferings.

The sacred cow is considerable for them as cow slaughtering is forbidden in their religion and they term it as "GAU MATA." Cow is scrutinized as a source of prosperity and goodness as its milk nourishes every creature. Although there are different perspectives in Hinduism regarding a vegan diet, according to a survey almost 9% of Hindus are vegans.

India is a pinpoint of many vegetarian schools and societies with 30% of the population practicing vegan lifestyle. This is the reason that the vegetarian South Indian Cuisine is so well developed. Mahatma Gandhi, founder of India, was a staunch follower of veganism and ate a meatless diet his whole life. He spread the message of ahimsa (non-violence), mortality, and veganism through his actions and stood by his vows.

Buddhism

The first doctrine of Buddhism is "not to kill." That forbids people from eating meat or any kind of fish. Buddhism adheres to veganism and considers that humans should not harm these living creatures in any case. Vegan

Buddhists succors to eliminate animal sufferings by not eating meat, eggs, fish, and other dairy products. Various Buddhist Monks are strict vegetarians as they believe that our bodies are temples and should be kept pure of other flesh.

However, another prejudice among Buddhist monks is to accept meat given as alms. Left-over meat or animal meals given as bounty are acceptable and can be consumed. The critics of this view give the perspective that meat given as charity or alms can also cause negative karma, as he gives the order to fetch, inflict, and kill the animal.

Another denomination in Buddhism writings claims that these animal spirits are a rebirth of our ancestors and fellows. Therefore, killing or eating an animal means we are eating the flesh of our mother, friend, or ancestors.

Among famous Buddhist scripts, there are some notable Buddhist texts in favor of veganism. The texts include:

· Mahaparinirvana Sutra
· Dhammapada
· Surangama Sutra
· Lankavatara Sutra

Gautama Buddha, the religious, spiritual, and mediator of Buddhism was a strict follower of the meatless diet. He also set forth for his disciples and followers to follow a plant-based diet. He spread the message that every plant-based or vegan edibles that have ever been cross-contaminated with meat should not be eaten or washed before consumption.

Today, many Buddhists consider vegetarianism as personal choice and do not find it compulsory to practice it. Though not all Buddhists have the same school of thought about practicing a vegetarian diet, a rough estimate states that half the Buddhists in the world are vegetarians.

Christianity

Christian veganism comes from a religious ascetic practice to eradicate cruelty or as an ethical consideration in a spiritual act to justify their position. Vegan Christians believe that veganism is closer to God's creation and design intent. They say that the Bible clearly states that animals are meant to be our friends and not our food. Animals and humans share the same breath and God's kingdom should be free from violence.

A great wrangle between vegan and non-vegan Christians is whether Jesus was a vegan or not. Although there exists no factual record of Jesus being a vegan, the message of kindness, grace, and mercy in Jesus's life developed a concept among vegetarians that his lifestyle clearly calls for pacification for lower ones.

On the contrary, meat-eating Christians hold the stance that the Bible teaches that humans are dominant over animals and can use them as food; there are no restrictions on using animals for food and products. Strict Greek Orthodox Christians follow a vegan diet for 40 days. During this time, they abstain from animal originated products, but these practices are just intended to be temporary. Moreover, Roman Catholics avoid animal flesh on Ash Wednesday, all Lent Fridays, as well as Good Friday. More and more Christian religious scholars and church leaders have begun to see consumption of meat as a sin, as it destroys our body, soul, and our Mother Earth.

Modern Christian vegans giving the message of following a vegan diet also have other motivations besides biblical references. People choose veganism because of the ferocity on animals. According to reports, animals are faced with brutal treatment in the food industry and on farms; examples include treatments such as culling of male chicks in the egg industry. Vehemence to animals is not reconcilable with a Christian world view.

THE ULTIMATE VEGAN DIET AND ALL THINGS YOU SHOULD KNOW ABOUT IT

What Actually Is a Vegan Diet?

The vegan diet is actually something quite restrictive. It starts from the animal flesh and ends with the animal-derived by-products. If you're thinking about starting a vegan diet, then you might be confused with the start-up. Before getting started with it, you should know the detailed viewpoints of the eating patterns.

No need to worry about your nutritional needs! Animal food has never been a necessity. The right choice of food is what you actually need.

What Do Vegans Eat?

The most common interrogation about veganism is about its technical description. Vegan diets include plant-based foods devoid of all animal products. Vegan menus involve all plant foods such as beans, legumes, vegetables, fruits, whole grains, and a wide range of plant-derived edibles.

Vegan foods repudiate the commodity status of animals; however, they have a diverse variety in vegan foods. Apart from the typical vegan diet, vegans may also choose to eat non-dairy yogurt, gelatin-free ice-cream and cakes, vegan macaroni and cheese, soy lentil veggie soups, carrot soba noodles, black bean and avocado meals, peanut butter and vegan creamy butternut with fried sage, veggie mayonnaise and spaghetti, hemp tofu (completely made of hemp seeds), veggie burgers, vegetable paella, stuffed sweet potatoes, humus Quesadillas, vegan lasagna, Thai red curry with vegetables, and a wide range of salads.

Nutritional yeasts and specific fermented foods are also favored in veganism. Tempeh is a protein-rich traditional food made of fermented soybeans. It has a distinct zest and nutty flavor and is made by a fermented process by which soybeans form a cake like tofu. Other famous vegan fermented foods include kimchi, kombucha, Sauerkraut, misso, natto, and zucchini relish.

FOOD TYPE	PROPERTIES	EXAMPLES
Fruits and Vegetables	Fruits and veggies are nutrient dense and particularly high in calcium and iron.	Leafy green vegetables such as spinach, kale, watercress, leaf lettuce. All fresh fruits such as berries, citrus, apples, etc.
Legumes	They act as a fiber-rich plant protein similar to meat, but are low in fats.	All sorts of beans, lentils and peas
Nuts	They have high fiber contents with lots of vitamins and minerals and can regulate body weight.	Walnuts, almonds, pistachios, cashews
Seeds	Seeds have omega-3 fatty acids and antioxidant properties.	Hempseeds, chia seeds, flax seeds

Whole grains and cereals	They are fiber-rich complex carbs with a high vitamin and mineral content of B-vitamins and iron.	Barley, white rice, brown rice, wheat, millet
Fermented Plant Foods	They contain probiotics and help in easier nutrient absorption.	Pickles, miso, kimchi, sauerkraut.
Dairy Alternatives	They have less calories with high water content to keep the body hydrated.	Soy milk, coconut milk, almond milk
Vegetable Oils	They have polyunsaturated and monounsaturated fats and help in cholesterol management along with CVD'S.	Soybean oil, corn oil, sunflower oil, canola Oil
Soy Products	They have a complete protein profile to meet the protein needs with low saturated fat.	Tofu, tempeh, seitan

There are many foods that are common for both vegans and non-vegans. Everyday similar edibles include banana bread, fries, fried beans, salad bowls, peanut butter, sandwiches, cornbread, and salsa. Vegetarian Thai curry and egg-free pasta with tomato sauce, vegan creamy sauce, and Thai sauce are often included in both diets.

RECOMMENDED FOODS IN VEGAN DIET

Vegan diet promotes all plant-based foods and it designed to fulfill a person's nutrient requirements properly. Dealing with the risk of nutrient deficiencies is a major challenge of this diet. As long as you're doing it right, then wipe away the fear!

Let's substitute all the animal products with plant alternatives. Here, we have listed all the allowed vegan items.

VEGAN- ALTERNATIVE FOODS

Alternatives for milk
Modern vegan diet plans make it easy to cut milk, cheese, and high-fat yogurt from your diet. A wide range of replacements are available for milk. There are alternative milks from rice, soy bean, nuts, seeds, and oats. Similarly, non-dairy yogurts are accessible for vegans and their

demand is increasing with time. Today, these non-dairy yogurts are available in many flavors.

Coconut oil and vegetable oil are used instead of butter in baking. Also, different butter substitutes are available with nutty flavors that give a whole new experience to baking. Moreover, avocado oil, canola oil, rice bran oil, grape seed oil, and light olive oils are widely used.

Substitutes for meat products

One of the most burning questions in veganism is "How do vegans fulfill their protein requirement?" Switching from a meat diet to plant-vegan diet causes protein

deficiency is a false claim; a vegandiet offers a diverse range of protein-rich foods.

Some whole and healthy vegan sources of protein include the following:

· Tofu or bean curd is a famous soy product. This chewy food is free of cholesterol and gluten and is an excellent source of iron and protein.

· Lentils, chickpea, black beans, and soybeans are a great source of vegan
protein.

· Seitan is a protein-rich food made from wheat. Seitan has a tangy taste, close to chicken in flavor, and has a meaty texture.

· Quinoa, seeds, and nuts are highly nutritious and credible sources of protein. Moreover, walnuts, hempseeds, and button mushrooms are also trusted protein inceptions.

Egg substitutes

A number of vegan foods have been introduced for egg replacements. Some of these replacements also work great in baking but some can be troublesome. However,  the choice of egg substitute in baking depends upon the recipe. The importance of eggs cannot be denied in terms of nutrition.

RESTRICTED FOODS IN VEGAN DIET

Staying away from all kinds of animal products is the key point and true purpose of a vegan diet. It is this simple! Adopting a vegan lifestyle is rewarding, but it comes with some challenges. Especially when you are a beginner and in a transition phase, a guide of do's and don'ts of a vegan diet must be considered.

To avoid some of the food items in a vegan diet is obvious and well known to you. However, there may be some food items that you should avoid, but you are not well aware of them. Here are the food groups and eatables that are restricted in a vegan diet.

FOOD TYPE	EXAMPLES
Meat	Beef, pork, lamb
Poultry	Chicken, duck, turkey
Seafood	Fish, crustaceans, shellfish Like mussels, shrimps, crabs, lobsters
Dairy Products	Milk, yogurt, cheese, cream
Bee Products	Honey
Other Animal derivatives	Whey, gelatin, casein, L-cysteine

Why these food types are bad?

Seafood

There is a possible reason as to why these foods are not allowed to be consumed in a vegan diet.

It is not so much about fresh sea fish as it is farmed fish that is the problematic element behind this. These farmed fishes that are labeled as sea fishes and put out in the market may suffer from different diseases. The aquamarine ecosystem these grow up in is also influenced by various drastic factors to begin with.

Sea fishes are considered hazardous to health because they absorb a certain concentration of the pollution in the ocean of heavy metals, plastic, and mercury that builds up in the bodies of fish in the form of methylmercury, which is highly toxic.

It has been scientifically proven that high levels of mercury, either direct or through dietary intake, can cause severe brain problems. A study was conducted in Brazil in which 129 adults were diagnosed with a high level of mercury in their body and showed elevated symptoms of memory loss, loss of attention, and poor motor skills. Moreover, it has been found that there

are certain ethnic groups vulnerable to having mercury toxicity as they consume a diet rich in fish rich. These groups include Native Americans, Asians, and Pacific Islanders.

Dairy

The main reason dairy is not allowed in the vegan diet is due to the fact that the gut is not able to digest the lactose and the amount of puss that drains into the milk due to oxytocin injections.

Poultry/Meat

This is unsafe because of the amount of antibiotics that are injected into the birds during farming and when they are transported. The World Health Organization (WHO) has declared meat as a "carcinogen" that leads to colon or rectal cancer. It's ultimately a bad idea to consume any type of meat whether its white meat, red meat, lamb, beef, or fish. Moreover, meat contains high levels of cholesterol and saturated fats, which are contributing factors to heart disease and diabetes.

Animal-derived Additives and Ingredients

Being vegan, you simply must quit any consumption of animal flesh. When you have chosen a purely vegan lifestyle, you should be aware of every ingredient in your food. Staying away from all kinds of animal products, including by-products, is the key point of a vegan diet. It is this simple!

Many times, you may not be sure about whether food is vegan or not, especially when it comes to derived products, food additives, preservatives, and ingredients.

Here are some of the animal-based additives that may be major ingredients of your daily consumption. Vegans should check the ingredient, nutrition, and food labels to make sure that they do not contain any of the ingredients listed below:

·Gelatin: Gelatin is a water-soluble and colorless protein usually obtained from animal tissues such as bone, skin, and connective tissues of pigs and cows

·Dairy ingredients: Lactose, Whey, and Casein are derived from animal dairy

·Shellac: Shellac is a lac purified by heating and filtering. It is usually used to make a food glaze usually in thin orange or yellow flakes but is sometimes bleached white for candy and other products.

·Vitamin D3: This vitamin is mostly derived from animals such as fish liver oil and the wool of sheep. For vegans, Vitamin D2 and Vitamin D3 alternatives are present in lichens.

·Flavorings: Several flavors that are added to food are animal-derived. For exam- ple, castoreum is a food flavor obtained from secretions of the beaver's anal scent gland.

·Additives: On food labels, many of the additives and preservatives are mentioned in short forms or represented with a specific alphabetic letter. It becomes difficult for one to recognize whether they are vegan or non-vegan. Some of the additives include E series: E120, E901, E904, E471, E422, E322, and E361.

·Carmine: This is a natural food dye used to impart red color also known as cochineal. Cochineal scale insects such as beetles are used to make this food dye.

·Isinglass: This is used in the making of beer and wines for coloring. It is a gelatin-like substance. Isinglass is derived from the bladders of fish.

IS THERE A DIFFERENCE BETWEEN VEGANS AND VEGETARIANS?

Vegetarians avoid eating flesh of animals but can eat eggs, dairy, and honey while vegans refrain themselves from eating all sorts of animal derived products and reduce animal exploitation. A vegan can be a vegetarian but a vegetarian can never be called a vegan.
In vegans, there might be some nutritional deficiencies as compared to the vegetarians due to restricted food items. However, this deficiency risk can be prevented by adapting the right vegan diet, along with the proper
nutritional recommendations. Vegetarianism can be easy and inexpensive but veganism is an ideal condition to survive. Both of these terms have major logical differences.
The main difference is that vegetarians don't eat animals and seafood, whereas vegan excludes all kinds of animals and animal-derived products like meat, dairy products, and honey. Vegans also do not utilize edibles that are processed using animal products such as wines and refined white sugar. These lifestyles are codified under various religious and ethical reasons. Other reasons may be health-related, environment-related, economic, or political.

Vegetarians: Vegetarians' diets have their roots as early as 700 B.C. A vegetarian diet involves abstaining from eating meat, fish, and poultry. Their diet includes vegetables, fruits, whole grains, nuts, eggs, dairy products, and honey.

A vegetarian diet may look like a pretty easy way to make the switch to eating more vegetables on a plant-based

diet, but it's important to note that there are different levels of vegetarianism.

There is a variation of diet among vegetarians:

·Lacto-vegetarian: Lacto-vegetarians avoids eating meat, fish, fowl, and eggs. Although, they will consume dairy products such as cheese, milk, and yogurt.

·Ovo-vegetarian: Ovo-vegetarians abstain from eating fish, fowl, meat, and dairy products. However, their dietary pattern includes consuming eggs.

·Lacto-Ovo vegetarian: Lacto-Ovo vegetarians are the most common type of vegetarians that do not eat any kind of meat and seafood. Further, their diet includes all kinds of dairy and egg products.

Vegans are strict vegetarians that exclude all types of animal food and animal-based products. Those who usually do not eat meat and poultry but do consume fish are referred to as Pescatarians, whereas flexitarians are part-time vegetarians or semi-vegetarians. Therefore, technically neither of these fall under the vegetarian category.

In ethics, vegetarians are opposed to the killing and slaughtering of animals, yet consider it acceptable to consume eggs and dairy products as long as the animals are kept in adequate conditions. They believe that animal products can be used as long as the animals are not harmed, injured, or slaughtered for human use. Vegetarianism is a bit less restrictive and thus easier to get a better intake of nutrients.

Vegans: The origin of vegan diets is a little more recent but are getting much limelight. Vegan society defines veganism as a lifestyle that attempts to exclude all kinds of animal exploitation and cruelty as much as possible.

Vegans are strict vegetarians that don't eat direct meat products or any by-products of slaughter. They eradicate all foods that have been made using processing aids from slaughter. Thus, they refrain from consuming eggs, meat, fowl, seafood, insects, honey, pepsin, albumin, gelatin, shellac, whey, and some forms of Vitamin D3.

Also, vegans do not use animal product fabrics such as leather, silk, and wool as they also have a large impact on animals and the environment. Vegans are also conscientious of cross-contamination which means that they may not eat food that has come in contact with any kind of animal food. Common vegan foods include cereals, oatmeals, fruit juices, vegetables, bread, veggie and lentil soups, salads, frozen fruit desserts, beans, macaroni, guacamole, chili, and spaghetti. Non-fat yogurt, candies having some gelatin content, and orange juices fortified with Omega-3 from fish are not consumed by vegans.

Vegan society believes that the greatness of a nation and its moral progress can be judged by the way its animals are treated. Vegans are of the view that animals are here with us, not for us to use them as snacks. Therefore, they have full rights to live free from human use, be it for clothing, science, food, or entertainment. Vegans hold the perspective that there is no fundamental difference between animals and humans in their ability to feel pain, pleasure, happiness, and misery.

HEALTH BENEFITS OF VEGAN DIET

People eat meat and think they become strong as an ox, forgetting that an ox eats grass. Nothing benefits human health and increases survival on earth as much as the evolution of the vegetarian diet. Veganism is not only a diet; it's about what we all need to have. Following a vegan lifestyle is associated with a bevy of health benefits.

Cardio-Benefits

Vegan diets are credited for lowering the risk of cardiovascular diseases.

A vegan diet decreases the blood cholesterol level, reduces the chance of heart disease, stroke, and various cardio disorders. Plant-based foods have zero cholesterol; however, omnivorous and most dairy foods have high levels of cholesterol that may clogs and harden the arteries. These foods have low sugars, low fats, low cholesterol, and low salt that would reduce the odds of heart attack, type 2 diabetes, and high blood pressure.

Vegan diets are the only diets proven to reverse and reduce heart strokes. People consuming more fruits and vegetables are at lower risk of death as compared to those with low consumptions. Polyphenols in plant-based products play a major role in improving cardio-health.

Weight loss

The vegan diet is increasingly becoming recognized as a healthier alternative to meat diets. Filling your plate with plant-based products will help you reduce body fat and weight. Fiber intake is key for losing body weight and vegan products are more focused on fiber content. Fiber consumption improves our clockwork bowel moments and boosts the digestive system. Eradicating animal foods from your diet means getting rid of unhealthy saturated fats.

A vegan diet would definitely help you shed some pounds as junk food is replaced with healthy whole food that is enriched with healthy fats. Vegan foods are rich in carbohydrates, giving you instant energy that helps boost your motivation for fitness. Considering the pros of a vegan diet, more fiber simply means more healthy body.

Protection against cancer

Starting a vegan diet is the best thing you can do for your health. Cutting animal products will reduce the risk of breast, prostate, and colon cancers. Vegan diets are less processed, less smoked, and are cooked at lower temperatures, thus reducing the risk of carcinogens. Plant diets have more soy products, which decrease the risk of breast cancer. Phytochemicals present in food and vegetables helps to protect against the damages caused by cancer. Consuming nutrient dense food, whole grains, legumes, and cutting down the processed meat and dairy products cut the cancer risks in half.

Glowing Skin

Increasing access to healthful foods fights stubborn pimples, controls acne, and improves complexion and skin tone. Getting a vegan diet not only improves your metabolism but the benefits will also definitely improve your skin. Fruits and vegetables have Vitamin C and E and selenium, which prevents skin cancers. Squamous cell carcinoma (SSC) risk is increased by eating meat and dairy, whereas a vegan diet helps reduce the risk of SSC. Surprisingly, dairy products cause skin breakouts and acne. Eating a vegan diet leaves you with healthy glowing skin. Root vegetables such as carrots and beetroots have B-carotene that boost anti-oxidant properties and gives a healthy glow. Additionally, soy foods increase the level of hyaluronic acid to help keep skin hydrated.

Improve kidney function

Dietary intake plays a significant role in the prevention and management of several kidney disorders. Consumption of soy protein leads to less hyper filtration and glomerular hypertension that preserves the efficiency of the kidney. Moreover, soy proteins reduces urinary nitrogen as compared to animal proteins.

Vegan diets will increase the level of insulin in the blood, thus reducing the sugar level and protecting from diabetic problems that can make kidneys worse. Eating plant-based foods will reduce the load factor on the kidneys as they are low in acids and fats. With kidney disease, excess phosphorus may harm bones but vegetable diets have less phosphorus to aid in improving kidney function. The alkalizing effects of plant-based potassium foods have explained reductions in metabolic

acidosis and kidney disease progression.

Cognitive decline

Cognitive decline refers to frequent confusions and memory loss, typically as symptoms of Alzheimer's disease and dementia. Plant dietary patterns exert neuroprotective effects. Vegan diets are rich in phytochemicals, polyphenols, anti-oxidants, and saturated fatty acids. Studies reveal that these compounds aid in the connection and survival of brain cells and boosts brain function.

Polyphenol-rich plant foods play a role in preventing Age-Related Cognitive Decline (ARCD) and improving cognitive function. Vegans have better self-control and interception as compared to those consuming an animal diet. Plant-based dietary supplements promote cognitive function and vegans show greater visual memory gains than meat-eaters.

Professor Koh Woon Puay, of National University of Singapore (NUS), conducted a study in his supervision and declared that dietary patterns impart a positive impact on mental health and cognitive impairment. He claimed that plant-based foods, i.e., vegetables, fruits, nuts, beans, and whole grains and the restriction of every single item of meat, especially if processed, is the key to stopping cognitive decline.

OTHER SOCIO-ECONOMIC BENEFITS OF A VEGAN DIET

Here are seven important benefits of vegan diets:
1. The vegan diet is considered beneficial for the conservation of the environment because no animals are being harmed in the process of doing so and no ecosystem is being destroyed.
2. The rights of animals are protected as they should be by nature. They are left free to live and breathe so the ecosystem can sustain its course and the terror of a species going extinct can be avoided.
3. A vegan diet is a friendly decision for animal lovers because they don't want to see animals suffer, or being decorated on a platter. It is more heartwarming to know that those animals are living in the forest or whatever landscape they are supposed to live, free from any type of harm whatsoever.
4. Middle class people have easy accessibility to vegan meals such as grains and vegetables as these are affordable.
5. Vegan diets significantly decrease the grocery budget due to it being an economical and cost-effective option.
6. Veganism excessively reduces the utilization of water.
7. Veganism saves the rainforest and decreases the carbon dioxide ratio.

THE PROTEIN QUESTION! WHERE DOES THE PROTEIN COME FROM IN A VEGAN DIET?

The topic of protein consumption by vegans has remained under heated discussions for a long time. A narrative that vegans are unable to fulfill their protein requirements is just a myth. Vegans get more than enough protein  from a vegan diet and it is not difficult for them to meet their protein needs. It is facile for a vegan to meet protein uptake needs as long as the intake of calories is ample.

Vegans are always shelled with a series of questions about protein consumption. The chief point is, 'How do vegans meet their protein essentials?' and 'Which vegan sources serve as protein reservoir?' There is no hidden enigma behind this; vegans just to have to consume a variety of food in adequate amounts. This section provides more detail about every aspect of vegan protein consumption.

What are proteins?

Proteins are large molecules and the building blocks of the human body. Proteins have high nutritional value and are essential for a number of life activities. Proteins are made of a linear chain of amino acids bounded together. Nearly 10,000 different proteins exist, which are made of 22 types of amino acids. Adults need eight essential amino acids in their body, whereas babies require nine essential amino acids for growth. Enzymes, hormones, antibodies, hemoglobin, and insulin are all proteins. Proteins proliferate hair, skin, bones, nails, and other different tissues.

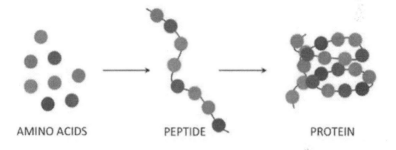

AMINO ACIDS   PEPTIDE   PROTEIN

One meal essential proteins

An American researcher named Frances Moore Lappe claimed that every meal you eat must consist of all eight essential amino acids. This narrative is still believed by some. On the contrary, it is said to be a myth and there is no obligation or condition that protein requirement of the body can only be met if we eat all eight essential amino acids at one time. Your body would not go deficient of protein due to a vegan diet until you are penniless or surviving on a single diet.

Digestion and absorption of protein in the human body either utilizes the protein readily or stores and converts it into various forms. Each and every cell in the body contains protein. Every second, numerous proteins are broken down and remolded to perform different functions. At the same time, different amino acids combine to form particular proteins according to the requirements of the body. The whole process takes place in the alimentary canal starting from the mouth going to the small intestine.

How to get proteins in a vegan diet?

To get proteins from a vegan diet, one must devour a wide range of vegan food. Consuming different types of food helps us in intake of all the essential amino acids that are not made by the body naturally.

Protein from vegetables

Veggies can serve as an easily available and inexpensive source of protein. In fact, vegetables can give you all kinds of essential protein if you eat a wide variety of them. Protein rich veggies include the following.

Watercress is a cruciferous plant that is protein rich. It's protein content is:

· One cup=0.8g protein

· Protein accounts for 84% of its calories

Alfalfa sprouts are the immature shoots of the alfalfa plant that are low in calories but rich in nutrients like protein.

· One cup=1.3g protein

· Protein accounts for 69% of their calories.

Spinach is considered the most-dense nutrient rich green leafy vegetable with good protein content.

· One cup=0.7g protein

· Protein accounts for 50% of its calories.

Moreover, edamame, broccoli, green peas, sweet potatoes, wild rice, Brussels sprouts, and fresh asparagus are also protein-rich vegetables.

Proteins from seeds, nuts and beans

There are plenty of protein-rich seeds, nuts, and beans that serve as protein reservoirs. Lentils, pulses, pinto beans, flax seeds, lima beans, soy beans, chickpea, Mung beans, fava beans, almonds, pistachios, and chia seeds.

Proteins from fruits

Fruits are a rainbow of nutrients. Apricot and guava have the most protein with more than 2g of protein per cup, whereas grape fruits, avocado, kiwi fruit, dates, berries, melon, and peach are also rich in proteins. Dry fruits are also protein-rich. Raisins give more than 3 g of protein per 100 gram. Prunes, a dry fruit, is also rich in protein.

Proteins from whole grain

Whole grains are known for their rich fiber content, but they also contain a handsome amount of protein. Whole wheat and brown rice contain a worthy amount of protein. Buckwheat, quinoa, and amaranth also provide a

decent amount of protein. Other protein containing whole grains include oats, millet, and cornmeal. According to a rough estimate, whole grains can fill 12% of your daily needs.

Plant Proteins for Athletes

Although veganism is getting much spotlight on social media, more and more
people from sports and games are taking interest in veganism but

there seems to be a lack of discussion for other athletes. Athletes should be guided through a detailed plan on how to build muscles and maintain their fitness levels following a vegan diet. High protein foods that help build muscles include pumpkin seeds, lentils, almonds, oats, tempeh, tofu, quinoa, and black beans. Today, plant-based protein powders are often used as an efficient replacement of proteins from dairy, meat, and eggs sources. Usage of protein powder in daily foods is recommended for vegan athletes. These plant based protein powders have proved to be quite efficient.

Moreover, for vegan athletes, plant derived protein supplements are also available for muscle and body building. These commercial plant based supplements comprise soy bean, rice, pea, hemp, and other protein products.

MISCONCEPTIONS ABOUT SOY PROTEIN

Soy is a high-level quality protein that comes from soybeans. Other rich sources are tofu, tempeh, soy milk, and soy sauce. Soy has been consumed extensively for centuries. It is power-packed with all the significant amino acids, minerals, vitamins, Omega-6 fatty acids, and Omega-3 fatty acids, with little saturated fatty acids and no cholesterol. However, many misconceptions and myths are spread about soy protein. It has become a common question of nutritional bloggers and the public whether soy is a super food or a sub-standard option. These myths have no scientific authentication.

Let's debunk the most common myths about soy:
  1. Is that true that men should not take soy?

It is believed that the intake of soy protein would reduce their testosterone level, enhance estrogen level, and would induce feminizing characteristics in them. This misconception is due to the naturally occurring estrogen in soy. Estrogen is considered a female hormone that plays a prominent role in sexual traits and development. It is said that this naturally present estrogen in soy promotes hormone imbalance in men and incorporates feminism in their body.

This allegation is incorrect. The natural estrogen present in soy is known as isoflavones, also classified as phytoestrogens or plant-estrogens. Scientists say that this estrogen does not function the same way as the estrogen hormone in females and this does not affect or reduce the testosterone level in men. Thus, soy has no effect on men's fertility.

Several kinds of research have also been conducted. The result of the analysis state that there is no effect from soy-protein, isoflavone, or plant-estrogen on testosterone or androgen levels. A Review of Fertility and Sterility in 2010 deduced that "Neither the isoflavone-rich soy nor the soy supplements affect free or total testosterone levels."

2. Soy escalates the risk of breast cancer in women.

There is no research-based evidence that proves that soy in women escalates breast cancer risk. The estrogen-like components are said to increase the growth of breast cancer. Breast cancers are sensitive to estrogen levels in the body and affect their growth; however, plant-based estrogen has no association with breast cancer. On the contrary, there are several studies and researches about soy that shows it actually prevents breast cancer. Breast cancer survivors who consumed soy in their diets reduced their risk of incidence. In a research analysis about breast cancer and soy consumption, 73,000

Chinese women were analyzed. Of those who consumed 13 grams of protein serving per day, 11% were at less risk of developing breast cancer than those who consumed less than 5g per day. Thus, soy has a protecting and preventing effect, or at the extreme, is said to be neutral.

IMPORTANT NUTRIENTS TO CONSIDER IN A VEGAN DIET

The word "Vegan" is finally getting much attention and this concept of veganism is spreading rapidly. An efficiently planned vegan diet is not only ethically good, but saves you from several diseases such as cardiac disorders and cancers.

An important concern about vegan diets is whether they provide your body with all the essential nutrients, minerals, and vitamins. Some interpret that a vegan diet is enough to fulfill all the nutrient needs of the body. Some are of the view that instead of using supplements, one should rely only on vegan diet plans. However, some vegan diets lack certain nutrients but thanks to vegan researchers and activists, we now have more than enough information about essential nutrients that play significant roles in our body.

The vegan lifestyle requires attention to nutrient consumption. As vegans do not eat animal products, honey, and gluten products, they need to keep a balance of nutrients for optimal health. Here are some of the nutrients that must be focused on with a vegan diet.

VITAMIN B12

Vitamin B12 is mainly found in foods of animal origin. Rich vitamin B12 foods include fish, eggs, meat, shellfish, and dairy products. Some believe that people following proper vegan diet plans have not to worry about the B12 deficiency, whereas it is a risk point if you are a strict vegan and not taking any kind of supplements. Vitamin B12 plays an important role in our body functions and metabolism:

·Vitamin B12 is involved in the formation of red blood cells that transport oxygen.

·It plays a significant part in protein metabolism.

·Affects the nervous system.

·Prevents anemia

·Deficiency can lead to heart disease

·Lack of Vitamin B12 can cause bone disorders

VEGAN FOOD SOURCES

To prevent the deficiency of B12 in the body, the following points must be kept in view:

●The best source is Vitamin B12 fortified foods.

●Fortified foods include fortified soy milk, plant milk, nutritional yeast, and cereals.

- Taking B12 supplements are also encouraged.
- Consuming Nori seaweed
- Taking Cremini Mushrooms

The recommended dose of Vitamin B12 by nutritionists is 2.4mcg per day for adults; during pregnancies, the required amount is about 2.6mcg per day. Vitamin B12 must be taken in small doses as they are best absorbed and metabolized in small amounts.

Therefore, before taking any kind of Vitamin B12 supplements it's better to know about B12 levels in your blood. Older adults in their 50's should start taking supplements according to the doctor's recommendations, as vitamin B12 absorption decreases with age.

VITAMIN D

Vitamin D is a naturally occurring fat-soluble vitamin that is present in a few foods and added to other foods known as Vitamin D fortified foods. The most important compounds of this group are Vitamin D2 and Vitamin D3. Vitamin D is mostly present in dairy products and sunlight.

Vitamin D regulates different body functions, including:

·Maintain bone health

·Enhance absorption of minerals such as calcium and phosphorus

·Boost immunity

·Influence mood

·Improve memory

·Help in muscle recovery

VEGAN FOOD SOURCES

- Vitamin D fortified cereals

●Fortified milk of soy, almond milk, rice milk

●Vitamin D fruit juices like orange juice

●Mushrooms

●Exposure to sunlight for at least 5 to 30 minutes every day.

Although sunlight is an important source of Vitamin D, it further depends upon many different factors like time of the day, angle of radiations, and color of skin.

Studies in Finland reveal that sunlight in the winter is not enough to meet the daily requirements of the body thus one should attain optimum Vitamin D through fortified foods and supplements.

The recommended dose of Vitamin D daily for children and adults is almost 15mcg per day or 600IU per day. Getting less vitamin D than recommended can lead to osteoporosis and more fractures with weak muscles. Rickets in children is also caused by a deficiency of Vitamin D.

OMEGA-3 FATTY ACIDS

Omega-3 fatty acids are categorized into two types:

»Essential Omega-3 fatty acids: These acids can be consumed from the diet as ALA (Alpha-Linolenic acid)

»Long-chain Omega-3 fatty acids: These are long-chain and called non-essential fatty acids as they are made by our body such as DHA (docosahexaenoic acid) and EPA (eicosapentaenoic acid).

These Omega-3 fatty acids play important structural functions in our body:

·Improve overall health

·Enhance brain functions

·Structural role in eyes

·Long-chain fatty acids reduce the risk of cancer, especially breast cancer

·Reduce the risk of inflammation

VEGAN FOOD SOURCES

●Fortified Omega 3
fatty acid food
from plant sources
●Seeds are rich in
omega 3 fatty acids
like Flax seeds, hemp
seeds, and chia seeds.
●Soybeans, walnuts,
and plant-
based oils.

●Omega-3 fatty acids supplements like oil-based omega supplement algae oil.

Experts recommend that the daily intake of Omega-3 fatty acids must be

200-300mg. Some studies reveal that the level of Omega-3 fatty acids is less in vegans and vegetarians as compared to those who consume animal products or are omnivorous. These levels can be maintained by consuming supplements of omega 3 fatty acids such as algae oil.

IRON

Iron is a mineral that is required by our body for proper functioning. It
is also involved in energy processes and metabolism. Iron in the
body is present in two forms:

»Heme iron: This iron is only obtained from animal products.

»Non-heme iron: This iron is found in plants.

Thus, vegans have to eat more iron-rich foods to compensate for the
lack of heme iron. For this, vegans must eat balanced iron-rich
foods daily as iron serves a lot of functions in our body.
These functions include:

·Chief role in the production of red blood cells

·Helps in oxygenation of the body by carrying oxygen throughout
the
human body

·Part of many proteins and enzymes

·Lack of iron can leads to anemia

VEGAN FOOD SOURCES

●Iron-fortified foods such as cereals
and bread

●Green Vegetables, peas, beans, and
spinach

●Fruits, dry fruits

●Plant milk

The recommended dose level of iron
for men is 8mg per day but for an
adult woman, this dose is increased to 18mg per day as women
need more iron due to their menstrual cycles. During pregnancy

duration, this dose is further increased to 27mg per day. Before taking any kind of iron supplements one must know the level of heme in the body and contact a doctor for the proper consumption of iron supplements.

CALCIUM

Calcium is a mineral that supports our skeletal structures. It makes up 1% to 2% of the body weight, out of which nearly 99% of calcium is present in teeth and bones. Calcium is not commonly deficient in vegetarians, but strict vegans with no dairy and dairy derivatives are at risk of being calcium deficient.

·Builds our bones and keeps them strong

·Strengthens teeth

·Needed for the muscles

·Role in nerves communication between different body parts

·Calcium deficiency can lead to serious bone disorders such as osteoporosis

VEGAN FOOD
SOURCES

Vegan-friendly food
sources of calcium
include:

●Calcium-fortified
foods: Fortified juices,
soy milk, almond milk,
cereals, bread, and rice milk

●Leafy green vegetables: kale, bok choy, turnip greens, broccoli, collard

- Beans: Chickpeas, black beans, mustard, soybeans, pinto beans
- Tofu and tempeh
- Nuts: Hazelnuts, Almonds, Pistachio nuts
- Calcium supplements

The Daily recommended dose of calcium for a vegan is 525mg. Vegans need less calcium as compared to meat-eaters as they do not need calcium to neutralize the acids in the body produced due to meat-eating. Calcium supplements are an easy way to consume and fulfill body requirements but levels of calcium in the body must be taken into consideration before taking any kind of supplements.

ZINC

Zinc is an element that is present in trace amounts in our body. It is the second most abundant metal in the body after iron. Vegetarians are at less risk of developing zinc deficiency as compared to strict vegans. Vegans should eat zinc-rich foods to meet the zinc requirements. Benefits of zinc include:

· Boost the immune system and fight off invading bacteria and viruses
· Formation of DNA and Proteins
· Growth and development of infants
· Faster wound healing
· Stimulates enzyme activity
· Deficiency can lead to hair loss, rough skin
· Lack of zinc can cause loss of taste and smell

VEGAN FOOD SOURCES

Vegans should be well aware of the plant sources that are rich in zinc as most plants have little available. The amount of zinc in plants also depends upon the zinc content of the soil in which they were grown. Here is a list of plant-based foods rich in zinc:

- Toasted wheat germ, firm tofu
- Lentils and Lima beans
- Seeds like chia seeds, hemp seeds, flax seeds
- Oatmeal, wild rice quinoa
- Green veggies like green peas and spinach
- Zinc supplements such as zinc gluconate

The daily value of zinc to be taken is 11mg. Taking Zinc supplements can fulfill more than 50% of the daily amount needed. On a whole, zinc is an important mineral that helps in the general body function.

PROTEIN

Protein is an essential nutrient of the body that is required in large amounts.

Protein is present throughout the body in muscles, proteins, skin, nails, and hair. Shortly, protein is an important component of every body part. Proteins have a high range of functions in the human body, including:

·Stimulates enzymes

·As a fuel, provides energy

·Powers chemical reactions of the body

·Makes up hemoglobin to carry oxygen

·Helps in making antibodies

VEGAN FOOD SOURCES

It is often assumed that vegans might have very few options for protein intake as meat is considered the most prominent protein source. Actually, the consumption of a proper plant-based diet can provide an excellent amount of protein. High protein foods include:

- Seitan
- Red lentils and green lentils
- Chickpeas, almonds, peanuts, and peanut butter
- Hemp seeds and chia seeds
- Quinoa
- Nuts and legumes
- Protein-rich veggies
- Protein-rich supplements

The daily recommended intake of protein is 0.8g of protein/kg of body weight and it calculates to almost 56g to 60g per day for an average person. If enough calories and proteins are taken in a day, your body will make its own complete proteins.

As a vegan, one can have a healthy lifestyle. However, this requires making balanced and healthy choices. Do not choose junk food options. Reading food and nutrition labels can help a lot in knowing the composition of each food item.

It is important to discuss your vegan diet plans with a doctor or nutritionist since vegan or vegetarians diets may be deficient in some minerals and nutrients. It is important to know about the diet portions and their consumption for the optimum intake of nutrients. Vegans who are suffering from a lack of some nutrients can use nutrient supplements to fulfill the body's requirements.

One should keep an eye on deficient nutritional symptoms and changes in weight, skin, and hair. Still, it's better to contact your doctor before following any diet plan.

VITAMIN A

Vitamin A is a fat-soluble micronutrient and comprises a group of organic compounds including carotenoid and retinal. Vitamin A is actively used by the body and is mainly found in meat products. But there are diverse options in the vegan diet for consuming Vitamin A. Vitamin A accounts for various functions in our body:

·Required for a healthy immune system and repel invading infectious organisms

·Key for good eye vision

·Boost metabolism of the body

·Cell growth

·Reduce acne and wrinkles

·Powerful anti-oxidant

·Prevents heart disease and cancer

·Keeps the linings of the lungs and digestive system healthy

VEGAN FOOD SOURCES

·Carrot and carrot
juices
·Spinach
·Sweet potatoes,
pumpkins
·Butternut squash and
orange juices
·Orange and Yellow
Fruits: Mango, melon,
apricots, tomatoes, and papaya

·Kale and watercress

The recommended daily intake of Vitamin A for women is 600mcg per day and for men, it's 700mcg per day. People age 19 to 24 years are at more risk of having a Vitamin A deficiency. A survey reports that almost 9% of women and 7% of men have Vitamin A deficiency worldwide.

TAURINE

Taurine is an amino acid that is important for several metabolic processes of the body. Usually, taurine does not lack in vegans but American research studies reveal that taurine levels in vegans are low as compared to levels in meat-eaters.

So, taurine should be paid special attention in vegan diet plans as it comprises 0.1% of body weight. Many biologically important functions are performed by taurine in the human body such as:

·Regulates cardiovascular functions and osmoregulation

·Essential for working of the skeletal and nervous systems
·Helps in antioxidation
·Plays role in calcium signaling and stabilization of membrane
·The body utilizes taurine for growth
·Used in repairing body tissues

VEGAN FOOD SOURCES

One can meet his taurine requirements from the following:
·Broccoli, Brussels sprouts
·Red peppers, garlic, onion
·Oatmeal, wheat germ
·Lentils, hemp seeds, quinoa
·Taurine supplements
The recommended daily allowance of taurine is 50mg to 2000mg. Even if taurine is taken in large amounts such as 3000mg per day, it is of no harm as the body stores taurine for later use. The human body itself produces taurine but to recoup it from diet and supplements, it is very necessary to keep your taurine level at an optimum.
It must be kept in mind that vegan and vegetarian foods don't contain enough taurine as required by the body.

WHY DO ATHLETES PREFER A VEGAN DIET?

As vegans eat only natural products and no fast food, they live a primarily healthy life which proves very beneficial for sportsmen and athletes. It helps them recover faster from workouts and they feel better in general. There is no inflammation in the body when following vegan diets, which is why athletes prefer vegan diets. Ahough more and more athletes are leaning towards becoming vegan, due to a lack of knowledge and literature, people usually give up on their idea. This book attempts to give you a complete overview as to why athletes should prefer vegan diets. It's time to bring a full stop to the idea that consuming a vegan or vegetarian diet while being a muscular and fit athlete is mutually prohibitive. Carl Lewis, winner of 10 Olympic medals, once said, "I decided to become a vegan in July 1990 and it was my best year as an athlete."

Vegan Athletes through the Ages

Donald Watson was the founder of the vegan society. Roman gladiators used a vegan diet as a part of their training programs. One of the famous Indian wrestlers from the late nineteenth and early twentieth century's also survived on vegan diets. Gama has the power to do thousands of push-ups and squats (Hindu) in a single session.

In 1870, great efforts were made in proving that vegan diets were far healthier than the diets that included meat. John Harvey of Kellog was the most vocal and famous promoter for vegan diets of that time. In the closing decades of the 19th century, a 62-mile running race was held. In this race, the first four of the eleven finishers were vegans. A 74-mile walking race was held in Germany in which six vegans achieved top-ten finishes in less than 14 hours. In contrast, no meat-eater ever won the race.

As word spread about the vegan athletes, researchers like Yale's Irving Fischer also took interest in it. From 1890 to 1900, Irving did a lot of research and experiments for comparing the power of vegans versus meat consumers. The results of these experiments suggested that low protein diets were potentially more advantageous than high protein diets. This challenged claims that a) vegan diets are less nutritious and b) vegans are not consuming enough proteins. Fischer's results were verified as scientific proof of veganism's benefits.

Vegan bodybuilders thrived about one hundred years ago. Two men were leading the way in this regard–Barrnerr Macfadden and Eustace Miles. In the early nineteenth century, Macfadden was one of the most popular renowned fitness personalities in America. His magazine *Physical Culture* had a readership of more than 100,000 in one year, from the end of 1899 to 1900. Similarly, physical culture books written by him were also in high demand in that era. Miles has particular importance in the story because of his publicized victories. In 1908, he won an Olympic Silver Medal at the ripe age of forty just because of his vegan diet. In his books, he told followers that his strength, endurance, and vigor were the result of his plant-based diet. In 1890, vegans also set Olympic records in swimming and tennis.

Vegan Diets Improve Athletic Performance

·A plant-based diet is low in fats and has no cholesterol.

·It helps in improving the viscosity of blood and its thickness.

·Vegan foods improve arterial flexibility and diameter, which lead to good blood flow.

·"The Game Changers" is a documentary that posits that professional athletes' performance can be improved by a vegan diet.

·Vegan athletes recover faster as vegetables enhance the ability of the
body to repair damaged tissues rapidly.

·Plant-based diets improve cardiovascular health, which is very important for any sportsperson or athlete (according to a recently published article in the journal).

·Those who eat a plant-based diet rich in whole grains have better bowel movements because these diets are rich in fiber, whilst dairy products and meat contain none.

Vegan diets help you lose weight, which is significant for athletes.

·The weight loss benefit of veganism also proves very helpful in gymnastics.

·Athletes of all levels, from youth to elite and recreational, can meet their nutrient and energy needs from eating vegan foods.

·Vegan athletes can do more exercise and they are less fatigued than non-vegan athletes.

·Vegan foods provide sufficient calories to athletes.

·Traditional bodybuilding requires large proteins that are efficiently provided by plant-based foods.

Advantages of Vegan Diets to Athletes

Following a vegan diet may benefit athletes in the physiological ways given below:

·It lowers saturated fats and promotes leaner body composition.

·Improves storage of glycogen in cells of muscles through carbs found in legumes, grains, and root veggies for high endurance.

·It increases oxygen and bloodflow in body tissues.

·It reduces oxidative damage in athletes.

·It decreases inflammation and makes the body's recovery very speedy after hard and intensive training of athletes.

·It protects the heart from risky factors of cholesterol and high blood pressure for the safe competition of athletes.

·New studies find potential health benefits for athletes eating vegan diets.

·Performance by vegan or vegetarian athletes are found to be two to three times better in terms of stamina, strength, and endurance.

·Marathon runtime of vegans is two hours faster than omnivorous athletes.

·Usage of medications, drugs, and medical supplies is less in vegans than in non-vegans.

·Dietary assessment of vegans was limited.

·The expectancy of lifespan increases and mortality is reduced.

·Low mortality rate from CVD

·A lower heart resting rate protects, improves, and maintains cardiovascular health.

·Total and daily intake of protein is sufficient.

·Recommended protein intake meets or exceeds suggested amounts.

·High quality proteins are obtained from plants and utilized by the body because these proteins provide all the essential amino acids needed by the body.

·Plant-based proteins are healthier than animal-based proteins because

they provide no saturated fatty acids and no Trans fatty acids.

·Vegan diets ensure good health of the gastrointestinal tract.

·It ensures good health of bones. There is no risk of osteoporosis or fractures in athletes because of the high density of minerals in bones.

·Good muscle health (metabolic activity and functional capacity).

·Few biological hazards.

·Complex carbohydrates in high amounts and nutrient density is naturally obtained by it.

·A high potential for alkalizing

·The diet is adequate from pregnancy to maturity and all athletes.

·It is less expensive than non-vegan foods.

·The health status of vegans and vegan athletes are always in the normal
range.

·Vegans are markedly less affected by chronic diseases.

Drawbacks of Eating Meat-Diet For Athletes

For a long time, animal diets have been considered best for an athlete's
fitness and health and many still believe that animal products like meat, fish, and dairy are critical and essential parts of their nutritional diet. Through research and extensive studies, it has been revealed that animal diets mostly focus on a single nutrient diet. For example, we all know that milk and dairy are a source of calcium, whereas, relative to fruits and veggies, milk contains scarce amounts of vitamins and minerals. It also contains some anti-nutrient factors such as an allergic protein. On the contrary, dark green leafy vegetables contain the same level of calcium as milk and are more easily digested. Moreover, the human body is not designed to eat meat. Carnivores and omnivores have short digestive systems and thus are suitable for eating meat. However, the human body has a long digestive tract that is better designed for eating plant-based diets.

·Digesting meat and animal foods demands a lot of energy and proves to be a stressor on the digestive system.

·Complex foods and a heavy diet like oil-fried meat and dairy requires a long digestive time.

·There are nearly zero carbs in the meat diet and thus nothing available to
fuel the body's performance.

·Eating red meat in more than a single meal causes a high risk of developing cancer. Consuming processed meat increases the risk of colorectal cancer by 20% to 30%.

·People consuming more meat tend to die earlier than vegans. Harvard studies claim that there is a connection between dying young and consuming more red meat. Vegans live an average of 83 years, whereas non-vegans have an average life span of only 72 years.

·Eating meat products and maintaining a lower BMI becomes difficult for an athlete. However, eating a vegan diet helps you in getting fit. Vegans are 10 to 20 pounds lighter than meat-eaters.

·Food poisoning is more likely associated with animal derived products.

Approximately 9% of all food poisoning results from eating beef.

·Consuming meat, eggs, and dairy increases the blood cholesterol level and slows bloodflow. It might also cause erectile dysfunction in men.

·Meat is a complex acidic food. It is stressful for the body to break it down and the kidneys have to work double. Athletes have to do more exercise regularly to burn meat fats.

·A famous line for athletes is "Just keep running." If you are a meat-eating athlete, you are going to lose your running power because the excess protein in meat leads to osteoporosis and weakening of bones.

Extremely high cholesterol levels, risk of cancer and diabetes, slow metabolism activities of the body, and sluggish digestive system are destructive to an athlete's body and future athletic success. Meat and fatty foods are to be broken down first, through the process of oxidation for which they have to consume carbs. No carbs mean no fuel to carry the process, so now what can one do, "hit the wall?"

Guidelines for Athletes

"The more intense the training, duration and time – the more important the diet is," says Larson Meyer, a professor in Food Program and Human Nutrition at Wyoming University.

It's true, whether athletes are training heavily competing for a triathlon, in the gym, martial arts, or sprints, all they need is a good dietary intake to keep their energy level up.

Following guidelines is very important for vegan athletes. They must follow these for best results:

· Vegan athletes should maintain their iron levels by eating whole foods from iron sources.

· They should reduce their consumption of foods that contain inhibitors like coffee, tea, and cocoa (when eating meals that are rich with iron).

· They should consume those foods concurrently with foods that contain Vitamin C.

· Athletes should be encouraged to take a diet that contains plant foods. It should include grain products, fruits, vegetables, and especially plant foods that are rich in protein.

· Being vegan, they should avoid all meat and animal-derived products like eggs, seafood, dairy, poultry, and even honey.

· To make the lifestyle of a vegan athlete more fueling, make sure to eat a diet that is rich in micronutrients like grains, nuts, seeds, and beans.

· Avoid foods that are processed and fermented. Do not indulge in junk food.

· Vegan athletes don't need more protein inherently. Vegan athletes don't need to take any supplements for proteins because if they eat proper vegan foods in the right quantity, the basic body's protein requirements are fulfilled.

· Drinking plenty of fluids is essential. Drink before, during, and after training sessions as dehydration can severely affect an athlete's performance, which can lead to electrolyte imbalance.

· A vegan athlete should switch up his meals with a variety of food to ensure the availability of all nutrients and elements.

· A competitive athlete should keep protein bars available. He should also keep a routine for food.

· Vegans usually eat fiber in large quantities. Drinking enough water can help them in preventing digestive problems.

· He should cut out all animal products and ingredients and swap out his favorite non-veg items for best results.

· Some type of bread may include ingredients that are not vegan such as honey, eggs, butter, and milk. The solution to the problem is simple; check the ingredients list to ensure that the product is purely vegan. In this regard, sprouted wholegrain bread should be considered.

Fifteen Healthy Foods that Vegans and Vegan Athletes Can Eat

Organic vegan athletes are blessed with a list of various foods options. The key to achieving a strong and healthy body only depends upon the balanced
intake of these nutrients and food items.

· Nuts, Seeds, and Nut Butters
· Legumes
· Chia seeds
· Plant milk which is calcium-fortified
· Plant yogurts which are calcium-fortified
· Flax and hemp
· Tofu

- Seaweed
- Nutritional yeast
- Sprouted plant foods
- Plant foods which are well fermented
- Whole grains
- Pseudocereals and cereals
- Foods which are rich in choline e.g., almonds, apples, bananas, and
whole wheat bread
- Vegetables and fruits

Fruits and vegetables are a complete package of a range of nutrients like iron, calcium, minerals, carbohydrates, proteins, fiber, vitamins, and fats. They have super nutritional worth and are better than any processed or fermented foods. Dried fruits, dates, and bananas are the best foods during training.

After a hard training session and hours of exercise, athletes have utilized all their glycogen stores. They need to restore all the lost glycogen to optimum levels. At this time, fruit shakes and smoothies prove to be the "Glycogen Window" for athletes.

Healthy Athlete Meals

Being an athlete means that you are constantly exerting yourself and thus require proper rest and a nutritious vegan diet to help you restore those muscle fibers. The most effective healthy meals that can help you with that might include vegan protein shakes (you can purchase the powder and vegan milk in order to make these delicious meals on your own), protein bars, as well as bananas because they are rich in potassium and can help in the restoration of muscular energy. You can make this decision on your own such as what will go best with your current training mode and the energy that you exert on a dedicated sport.

MODERN RESEARCH CONCLUSION ABOUT VEGAN ATHLETES

All modern research about vegan diets and their impacts on the performance of athletes reveal that athletes must adopt vegan foods and dietary plans to stand out from the crowd and for high endurance, vigor, strength, and power. Although it has a limited amount of drawbacks, all the research scientists and their experiments conducted to compare vegans and non-vegans promote the vegan dietary plans and foods directly or indirectly. According to the ADA (American Dietetic Association), vegan food is nutritionally suitable for all life stages of athletes.

Veganism is a life choice that more people are choosing. Over the last few years, well known international athletes and sports stars also made the decision to follow a vegan lifestyle. This trend is increasing day by day and will likely continue to do so.

20TH CENTURY POPULAR VEGAN ATHLETES

Many professional athletes have carved their way to success by adopting a vegan lifestyle. The following are international elite athletes who adopted veganism:

1. Carl Lewis - He won nine Olympic medals in Track & Field.

2. Martina Navratilova - Tennis player with 18 Grand Singles titles and 31 Doubles titles (still a record).

3. Robert Parish - A basketball player over seven feet tall!! 2003 Hall of Fame.

4. Brendan Brazier - Professional Ironman, two times Canadian Champion,

2003 and 2006 National Marathon Champion.

5. Bill Pearl - Bodybuilder, four times Mr. Universe.

6. Venus Williams - Tennis

7. Jermain Defoe - Soccer

8. David Haye - Boxing

OBSESSION AND HAZARDS OF ANIMAL PROTEIN

Many people are obsessed with animal protein, making health as their basis, whereas it is proved by facts that at some point, animal protein is damaging and causes several diseases in humans. Diets rich in animal protein are not good for human health, especially those protein foods that are cooked at high temperatures. Dr. Campbell of China, after 25 years of research, claimed that many of the carcinogenic issues are related to casein protein. This is one of the major proteins in dairy. Explaining further, he said that people obsessed with animal food would make every possible effort to keep animal meat and dairy in their diet, ignoring the fact that their saturation can cause serious damages to their body.

Hazards of animal protein

Animal protein is directly or indirectly related to various diseases and disorders of the human body. Its imbalance consumption causes:

- Accelerated aging
- Kidney stones and other kidney disorders
- Obesity in children
- Skin problems like acne
- Female infertility
- Premature puberty
- Bone disorders
- Premature death, diabetes, cardio-disorders, and cancer

DIFFERENT TYPES OF VEGAN DIETS

Vegan diets are becoming more popular every day. Vegans do not eat meat and eradicate all animal products from their diet to avoid cruelty. Vegan diets offer a wide variety of food, and there as many ways of enjoying a vegan diet as for non-vegan diets. Different types of foods seems sensible to different people but you have to make an educated choice according to your body.

There are pros and cons to every different type of diet. Different types of vegan diets are mentioned below:

1. Whole-foods plant diet
2. Raw vegan diet
3. Starch solution vegan diet
4. Nutritarian vegan diet
5. 80/10/10 raw low-fat vegan diet

6. Detox vegan diet

7. Junk food vegan diet

8. Raw till 4 diet

9. Plant diet SOS-free

10. Low-fat whole starch vegan diet

11. Low-fat high-carb vegan diet

12. Esselstyn heart-healthy vegan diet

13. Engine 2 diet

14. Low-carb vegan diet

15. Strict vegan only plant diet

Let's get into the essentials of these distinct diets.

WHOLE FOOD PLANT DIET

The whole food vegan diet includes all the basic plant-based food groups. More than a diet, it's a lifestyle. The whole food vegan diet provides a maximum of nutrients as all these food groups are nutrient-dense. This diet mostly focuses on eating unprocessed foods.

Popular foods:
Whole grains
Legumes Fruits Vegetables Nuts
Seeds

Benefits:
- Lower risks of cancer (prostate cancer and breast cancer)
- Prevent chronic disorders
- Help lose weight
- Prevent and treat diabetes
- Increase life years
- This diet is quite flexible with a diverse range

Example meals:
- Mango smoothie
- Veggie curry
- Vegetable pasta
- Oatmeal
- Cereals
- Green tea
- Mashed sweet potatoes
- White bean avocado toast

RAW VEGAN DIET

Raw foods are kept as simple as possible. These foods are not cooked at high temperatures as it might destroy their nutrition. Different raw foods are eaten at a different level of rawness depending upon the choice and need.

Popular foods:
- Nuts and seeds
- Fruits and dry fruits
- Vegetables, especially leafy green vegetables that are eaten raw
- Sea vegetables

- Soaked and sprouted grains
- Soaked and sprouted legumes
- Edible forms of algae

Benefits:
- Highly nutritious
- High fiber diet that improves intestine function
- Lower risk of diabetes
- Lessens risk of cardiac disorder
- Improves digestion
- Less risk of obesity

Example meals:
- Soaked quinoa
- Sprouted lentils
- Raw tofu
- Almond milk and unroasted raw nuts
- Chia seeds
- Banana
- Kale salad
- Raw carrot cake
- Mushroom burgers

STARCH-SOLUTION VEGAN DIET

Starch-based diets mainly emphasize on eating plant-based starch-rich foods with no oils. This diet uses the least processed food with limited sugars and salts to keep the food palatable. It is claimed by Dr. John McDougall, that one could eat potato (highly rich in starch) for months and stay healthy.

Popular foods:
· Whole grains like wheat, rice, maize, barley
· Starch-rich veggies such as potatoes
· Non-starchy veggies are also recommended as broccoli
· Grains such as brown rice and quinoa
· Fruits should be taken in fewer servings and not considered as a meal

· High dietary foods like nuts, seeds, and avocados taken in the least
amount

Benefits:
· Rich in fiber
· High nutrients
· Lessens the risk of chronic failure
· Reduces obesity
· Compliant foods

Example meals:
· Potato smoothie
· Lima bean salad
· Rice with beans and chili
· Low-fat mushroom salad

· Chocolate oats

NUTRITARIAN VEGAN DIET

The idea of the nutritarian vegan diet was coined by Dr. Joel Fuhrman. This diet limits starch-rich foods and encourages the intake of nuts and seeds. The nutritarian diet is gluten-free and has low sodium and low fats. It requires you to eat more nutritious food and lessen processed foods including oils and sugars.

Popular foods:
You have to eat a lot of
G.B.M.O.B.S
· G: greens
· B: beans
· O: onions
· M: mushrooms
· B: berries
· S: seeds

Benefits:
· Lower blood pressure
· Lower sugar level
· Lower cholesterol
· Suitable for weight loss

· Enhance longevity

Example meals:
· Veggie wraps
· Beanball noodles
· Fruit pudding
· Chia pudding
· Lentil salad
· Zucchini noodles

80/10/10 LOW-FAT RAW VEGAN DIET

This diet plan was created by Doug Graham. Graham who was an athlete and a doctor, wrote a book on this low-fat raw vegan diet. According to him, the perfect ratio of nutrients in a healthy diet must be:

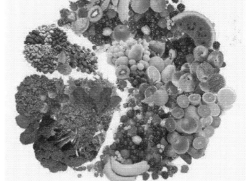

· 10% proteins
· 10% fat
· 80% carbohydrates

Huge portions of ripe, organic fruits and vegetables are eaten. People are likely to pursue this diet, especially those living in hot climates. On a lighter note, this diet is known as "Fruitarianism." Drinking a lot of water and eating only one type of food or meal (mono-meals) is highly recommended. However, the use of salt is highly discouraged.

Popular foods:

· Fresh and organic fruits such as berries, bananas peaches, apples, oranges, dates, melons

· Avocado, cucumbers

· Leafy green vegetables, lettuce, spinach

· Few nuts and seeds

· Olives

Benefits:

· Decrease obesity risks

· Increase longevity

· Reduce the risk of type 2 diabetes

· Lessen risks of cancers, chronic disorders

· Reduce depression

· Reduce blood sugar

· Reduce blood pressure and blood cholesterol levels

Example meals:

· Green smoothie

· Low-fat soups

· Zucchini pasta

· Bowl of cucumber and savory fruits

· Mango or berry banana meals or smoothies

DETOX VEGAN DIET

The detox vegan diet is conceptualized to clean your body. Our body is working day and night to detoxify the toxic foods we put in our body. Although switching from an animal diet to a plant diet reduces the number of toxins in a large amount, still, the intake of junk food and carbs causes stress on the body's metabolism. So, eating a

detox vegan diet will clean up your body

from toxins, give you a healthy nutrient-dense diet, and fuel up your cells for further metabolism. The detox vegan diet is antioxidant rich and reduces the oxidative stress.

Popular foods:
· Soaked nuts and seeds
· Fresh vegetables
· Organic leafy and non-leafy vegetables
· Legumes, beans, lentils
· Brown rice
· Filtered water
· Oils like olive oil, coconut oil

Benefits:
· High fiber in this diet will flush toxins out of the body
· Clear glowing skin
· Less obesity
· Detoxify colon and liver
· Purifies blood

Example meals:
· Red and green smoothies of grapefruit and leafy green vegetables
· Beetroot patties and salads
· Vegetable soups
· Turmeric smoothies

- Ginger cookies
- Vegan salads with fresh tomatoes
- Red juices such as apple juices and carrot juice
- Non-roasted almonds

JUNK FOOD VEGAN DIET

Junk food vegan diet followers eat processed foods as long as they do not come from animals. The junk food vegan diet is necessary because the body requires those saturated fats occasionally for normal synergistic functioning, but other than that, it is not encouraged. However, junk food is not at all healthy but at least healthier than animal junk food of beef and chicken ingredients.

Popular foods:
- Vegan cookies and candies
- Fruit cakes and cookies
- Cereal products, legumes, nuts
- Veggie and cheese products
- Bread, pasta

Benefits:
- Increases transition
- Creates awareness about vegan food that vegans do not only live

on
salads
· Fulfills cravings

Example meals:
· Vegan pizza
· Vegan fries
· Vegan burger
· Cheese veggie sandwiches
· Chocolate fudge cake gluten-free
· Soy sauce pasta

PLANT-DIET SOS FREE

Dr. Alan Goldhammer gave the idea of an SOS-free diet. SOS stands for "Sugar, oil, and salt." The SOS-free diet is basically the eradication of oils, salts, and sugars from the diet. This diet is quite successful for weight loss as removing salt and sugar from food makes it less palatable and people eat less. Following this diet, one should also eradicate drugs, alcohol, caffeine, and tobacco.

Popular foods:
· Raw fruits
· Fresh vegetables
· Gluten-free whole grains (best recommended)

- Less processed foods
- Lentils and beans
- Some seeds and nuts

Benefits:
- Reduce the risk of diabetes and cancer
- Less risk of cardiovascular disease and stroke
- Helps stress management
- Suitable for weight loss
- No risk of kidney dysfunction

Example meals:
- Oatmeal
- Avocado and grapefruit salad
- Corn tortillas
- Mashed potatoes
- Salt-free lentils
- Fresh fruit salad with fresh mint
- Rice with corn

LOW FAT-WHOLE STARCH VEGAN DIET

Alex and Kristen of Los Angeles, also known as Mr. and Mrs. Vegan popularized this diet through social media. They claim that eating a simple and healthy diet with a little fun on the weekends keeps you more active. According to Mr. and Mrs. Vegan, eating only whole grain foods or only high-carb foods can make you weak and leads to stress and anxiety problems.

Popular foods:
- Legumes such as beans and lentils must be added

- Potatoes, pumpkins
- Corn, quinoa, brown rice
- Different variety of vegetables
- Fruits mostly as dessert or snacks

Benefits:
- Lower blood pressure
- Lower cholesterol level
- Decline chance of arthritis

Example meals:
- Veggie lasagna with sauce
- Oatmeal
- Colorful salad bowls
- Blueberry muffins

LOW-FAT HIGH CARB VEGAN DIET

This diet mainly focuses on high intake of carbohydrates, thus motivates you to consume
more nuts, dry fruits, and seeds which at
times can be difficult. This diet prohibits the use of oil and salt. However, sometimes people following this diet can gain weight as it is a high carb diet plan. This plan refers to more starch intake and is somewhat similar to the starch solution diet. This diet boosts weight loss and speeds up metabolism as it promotes low fat foods. Moreover, researchers observed that this diet burned 14% of the calories right after the meal because a high-carb diet demands enough energy to digest the food.

Popular foods:

- Whole grains and starch cereals
- All types of vegetables
- Fresh fruits
- Dry fruits
- Legumes
- Lentils that are rich in starch
- Bread, rice, cereals
- Seeds and nuts

Benefits:

- Prevent chronic diseases
- Low risk of diabetes
- Low risk of stroke and heart attack
- Helps you gain weight if you are skinny and weak

Example meals:

- Oil-free sweet potatoes
- Salad
- Bean burritos
- Pasta
- Pizza rolls

ESSELSTYN HEALTHY VEGAN DIET

Dr. Cadwell Esselstyn created the idea of a heart-healthy vegan diet. He wrote a book in 2007 regarding a heart diet to "prevent and reverse heart disease." This diet is highly recommended for those who want to prevent heart disease and strokes. Esselstyn said that a heart attack is not a disease and can be controlled by a low fat-diet. This diet plan includes cutting all animal products, oils, avocados, nuts, and soybean.

Popular foods:
· Unprocessed whole grains and cereals
· All kind of legumes
· Vegetables, except for avocados
· Fruit (avoid fruit juices as they boost triglycerides)

Benefits:
· Lower cholesterol level
· Prevent heart disease
· Lower blood sugar level
· Lower blood pressure

Example meals:
· Kale and cucumber sandwiches
· Lentils soups
· Broccoli and potato casserole
· Low-fat pumpkin muffins

ENGINE 2 DIET
The Engine 2 diet highlights whole-grain

plant-based foods and maintains fats at a low level, whereas a little space is there for some junk food. This diet plan was created by one of the offspring of Esselstyn named Rip Esselstyn. He planned a low-fat diet for his friend who was suffering from high cholesterol. Following his diet, he and his friend lost many pounds and were successful in lowering the blood cholesterol levels. The Engine 2 diet is quite famous. Its products are available in the market.

Popular foods:
- Whole grains and whole grains products like bread and pasta
- Vegetables, especially green veggies
- Dry fruits and fresh fruits
- Legumes and lentils such as black beans
- Nuts, seeds, and nut butter

Benefits:
- Prevent chronic conditions like heart attack and cancer
- Prevent diabetes
- Reduce weight
- Lower blood cholesterol level
- Lower blood sugar level

Example meals:

- Hummus veggie pizza
- Veggie burgers
- Blueberry pancakes
- Vegan oat bars

LOW CARB VEGAN (KETO) DIET

The low carbohydrate vegan diet or keto diet is very low in carbohydrates but high in fats and proteins. Following this diet, one has to eat a lot of vegetable oils and fats. Avoiding staple food as much as possible is recommended as they have high carb content. This diet usually contains a ratio of 25% to 35% fats and 30% proteins.

Popular foods:
- Non-starchy vegetables and vegetable oils
- Soy derived products
- Nuts, legumes, and nut butter
- Fruits, mostly berries

Benefits:
- Blood sugar control
- Support better athletic performance
- Lose weight
- Lower blood pressure

· Reduce acne and risk of cancer

Example meals:
· Avocado smoothie
· Steamed vegetables
· Tofu
· Lettuce wraps and garlic sauce
· Veggie mushroom soup
· Gluten-free chocolate mousse

JUST A VEGAN/PLANT DIET

These are plant-based eaters without any strict advice or guidelines. They omit only animal products but eat every kind of vegetable, oils, sugar, and vegan processed foods. They are simply just plant-eaters eating healthy vegan foods.

Popular foods:
· Grains and legumes
· Fruits
· Vegetables
· Packed and processed foods like oils and sugar
· Lentils, nuts, and seed
· Anything that is vegan!

Benefits:
· Boost immune system

- Reduce inflammation
- Lower blood pressure
- Stabilize sugar level

Example meals:
- Carrot and pumpkin cakes
- Strawberry and mango smoothie
- Vegan lasagna
- Vegan pizza and burgers
- Sweet potato salad
- Sandwiches with cashew cheese

More Variations/Types of Vegan Diets

Here are some other diets similar to the above-mentioned plans:

1. China diet
2. Biblical diet
3. Hallelujah diet
4. Macrobiotic diet
5. Popper diet
6. CHIP program
7. Natural hygiene diet
8. Kempner rice diet

Food Diets to be selected carefully:

· Soy-free vegan diet
· Sugar-free vegan diet
· Gluten-free vegan diet
· Oil-free vegan diet
· Wheat-free vegan diet
· Nut-free vegan diet
· Grain-free vegan diet

Concluding the overview of the topic, there are several vegan diet plans and styles. The best diet is the one that suits your body and health. So, do some research and cherry-pick the best diet plan for you.

WHY YOU SHOULD BECOME A VEGAN

The only regret in my life about being vegan is not going vegan earlier. The best advice I could give someone is to go vegan. I am a Vegan and it really feels good.

Going vegan is a great opportunity to know about more healthy diets and nutrition. Some people believe that the vegan diet is detrimental, unhealthy, unnatural, and impossible–all of these are fake perspectives. Naturally, our stomach is made for vegan foods not for meat foods. We have low bile content and a long digestive tract system, which is more appropriate for greens.

Veganism will not fix all of your problems, but it can be important for a solution. Meat and dairy indeed nourish our bodies, but at the same time, they are posing harmful stress and diseases on the body.

If one is struggling against obesity, inflammation, diabetes, and cardiovascular diseases then veganism is the first step to your success. It's quite easy to maintain an optimum weight when you are not eating cheese, heavy fat milk, beef, and chicken.

Asking for a healthy diet from nutritionists and health experts, you will always get the answer, "Eat more fruits and vegetables." No one will ever say to eat more beef and chicken, because these things are destructive for health and likely to kill more people early. One should only meat if it's healthy; if you think it is, then eat it. However, in previous years there have been tons of research done on vegetarians and there are mountains of evidence in favor of vegan diets. Veganism enlightens a diet with vitamins, minerals, carbohydrates, proteins, healthy fats, and antioxidants.

Veganism is an ethical progression. Veganism is not about leaving all your goods. It's about gaining more peace, satisfaction, and tranquility that comes from embracing pacifism and refusing to become violent. Veganism is a powerful step that you can take in making yourself and this world better.

Eat better! Feel better!

SCRUMPTIOUS VEGAN RECIPES THAT YOU MUST
TRY
AS A BEGINNER OR A STRICT VEGAN

CREAMY VEGAN PASTA

INGREDIENTS

FOR PASTA SERVING:
- 2½ cups shell pasta (small)
- 2 tablespoons extra-virgin olive oil
- 1 chopped small onion
- 5 cups broccoli florets along with chopped leaves
- ¼ cup toasted nuts
- lemon wedges

FOR CREAMY SAUCE:
- 2 cups white beans cooked, drained and rinsed
- ½ cup vegetable broth or more to taste
- 3 tablespoons squeezed lemon juice
- 2 1/2 tablespoons extra-virgin olive oil
- ¼ cup active yeast powder
- 1 minced garlic clove
- A pinch of onion powder
- ½ teaspoon salt
- Black pepper to taste

DIRECTIONS

Boil the pasta as per the package instructions. Stir broccoli florets and chopped onions in a greased pan. Prepare the creamy sauce in a blender with white beans, broth, minced garlic, active yeast, salt, black pepper, and lemon juice. Transfer the boiled pasta to a serving dish, add broccoli and onions over the dish, and drizzle it with creamy sauce. Garnish it with nuts of your choice along with lemon wedges.

VEGAN CHICKPEA FALAFEL

VEGAN CHICKPEA FALAFEL

INGREDIENTS

FOR FLAFEL:
- 1 cup uncooked chickpeas (must be soaked 24 hours, drained and rinsed)
- ½ cup chopped red or yellow onions
- 3 minced garlic cloves
- 1 teaspoon lemon zest
- 1 teaspoon ground cumin and 1 teaspoon ground coriander
- ¾ teaspoon sea salt
- ¼ teaspoon cayenne pepper and ¼ tsp. baking powder
- 1 cup chopped fresh parsley and cilantro leaves patted dry
- 1 tablespoon extra-virgin olive oil or more to drizzle

FOR SERVING:
- Pita bread
- Hummus
- Chopped tomato, cucumber, and pickled red onions
- Fresh herbs, chopped parsley, and fresh mint leaves
- Tahini Sauce

DIRECTIONS

With a food processor, blend the chickpeas along with all

the falafel seasonings in it. Create patty shapes with the prepared smooth mixture and bake them in a greased pan at 180 degrees.

Transfer the baked patties over the pita bread and then place the veggies and pickled red onions. Drizzle the tahini sauce over the prepared falafel and then sprinkle it with herbs. Note: Do not use canned chickpeas as the falafel will turn out mushy.

SWEET POTATO CURRY

SWEET POTATO CURRY

INGREDIENTS

FOR THE CURRY PASTE:
· 1 tablespoon coconut oil
· 1 chopped onion
· 2 minced garlic cloves
· 3-inch long grated ginger
· 3 tablespoons Thai red curry paste (make sure its vegan)
· 1 tablespoon peanut butter
· 500g peeled chunks of sweet potato
· 400ml coconut milk
· 200g spinach
· 1 tablespoon squeezed lemon juice
· Boiled/garlic rice to serve
· Roasted peanuts to serve
· Fried onions to serve

DIRECTIONS

Use a non-stick frying pan. Stir chopped onions in a greased frying pan over medium heat and then add minced garlic cloves and ginger. After frying for 2 minutes, add Thai curry paste along with peanut butter, coconut milk, and water. Mix well and add sweet potato chunks. Continuously boil the potatoes in the paste until they become soft. Next, add spinach and lemon juice to the curry. Serve the potato curry with plain boiled rice or garlic rice. You may garnish it with peanuts or crispy fried onions.

VEGAN SAUSAGE ROLLS

VEGAN SAUSAGE ROLLS

INGREDIENTS

FOR SAUSAGE ROLLS:
- · 300g chestnut mushrooms
- · 3 tablespoons extra-virgin olive oil
- · 2 finely chopped leeks
- · 2 minced large garlic cloves
- · 1 tablespoon chopped sage leaves
- · 1 tablespoon brown rice miso
- · 2 teaspoon Dijon mustard
- · 50g finely chopped chestnuts
- · 80g white breadcrumbs (fresh)
- · 1 x 320g ready to roll puff pastry
- · Plain flour for dusting
- · Soy milk or any other dairy-free milk

DIRECTIONS

Finely chop the mushrooms in a food processor. Fry the leeks in an olive oil greased frying pan until golden brown and sprinkle it with salt. Fry the mushrooms in it and add garlic, sage leaves, brown rice and Dijon mustard. Mix well and add chestnuts and white bread crumbs to get a stiff but smooth mixture. Dust the surface with some flour and unwrap the pastry sheet over it. Spread the mushroom mixture in the middle of the pastry and then roll it in a sausage shape. Cut the pastry into 2–inch pieces, brush them with milk, and then bake for 30 min GAS6/200C until golden brown.

PROTEIN SMOOTHIE JEREMY'S SPECIAL

FROZEN SMOOTHIE – JEREMY'S SPECIAL

INGREDIENTS

· 30g of vanilla vegan protein
· Half a ripe banana
· 2 spoon full of cacao
· 300 ml of unsweetened almond milk
· 2 big spoon fulls of sprouted oats
(depends how much carb you want)
· 1 spoon full of chia seeds
· 1 tea spoon of peanut butter

DIRECTIONS

In a blender, add vanilla vegan protein, ripe banana, cocoa powder, almond milk, and peanut butter. Blend everything well and then add sprouted oats at the end.

STEM+ GLORY VEGAN CONTRIBUTION

(Some Lovely Recipes)

I'm very honored that Stem + Glory shared their best recipes with me and now I am sharing them with you. Fuel your soul with some delicious plant-based foods.

CAULIFLOWER BUFFALO WINGS & RANCH DIP

CAULIFLOWER BUFFALO WINGS & RANCH DIP

INGREDIENTS

FOR THE CAULIFLOWER:

1 large head cauliflower

1 cup milk alternative

¼ cup apple cider vinegar

1 cup all-purpose flour

1 tablespoon garlic powder

FOR THE DIP:

½ cup vegan mayo/coconut Yogurt

1 tablespoon chopped parsley

1 tablespoon chopped dill

1 tablespoon garlic powder

1 teaspoon black pepper (to taste)

1 teaspoon sea salt (to taste)

1 tablespoon smoked paprika powder

½ tablespoon chili powder

½ tablespoon Cumin powder

½ tablespoon black pepper

1 teaspoon sea salt

Hot sauce/BBQ sauce to glaze

DIRECTIONS

Preheat a frying pan with oil at 180c on electric stove. Cut cauliflower into bite sized pieces. In a large bowl, add milk, apple cider vinegar, flour, garlic powder, smoked paprika, ground cumin, chilli powder, black pepper, and salt. Add the cauliflower to the batter in the bowl, and toss to combine. Remove the pieces of cauliflower and tap off the excess batter a few times on the side of the bowl. Place on a plate for getting ready to be fried. Fry in oil for 3 minutes. Flip them over and fry for 2 more minutes, until golden brown. Take out and place on paper towel to remove excess oil. Brush the BBQ sauce/hot sauce on each cauliflower wing, or toss the florets with the sauce in a large bowl, then place on the serving plate.

Place the vegan mayo/coconut yogurt in a bowl, mix in with the whisk (garlic powder, black pepper, sea salt) then add the chopped parsley and chopped dill. If you're using coconut yogurt, add 2 tablespoon of apple cider vinegar.

LASAGNE WITH CASHEW
BECHAMEL

LASAGNE WITH CASHEW BECHAMEL

INGREDIENTS

FOR THE LASAGNE:

Lasagne

courgettes cut into small cubes

1 aubergine cut into small cubes Olive oil

½ teaspoon dried oregano

1 celeriac, peeled and very thinly

Tomato sauce

litre passata

tablespoons tomato

paste 1 clove garlic (optional)

1 tsp dried oregano

½ teaspoon dried basil OR handful chopped fresh basil

FOR THE BECHAMEL:

1 cup cashew nuts, soaked 6 hours

1 cup water

¼ cup Engervite nutritional yeast flakes

½ teaspoon smoked paprika

½ teaspoon of salt (or more to taste)

Salt + pepper

DIRECTIONS

Drizzle the courgette and aubergine cubes in olive oil, add the oregano and season with salt and pepper. Place in a baking tin. Toss the celeriac sheets in olive oil and season well with salt and pepper. Distribute evenly in a large baking tin. Place both tins in the oven and cook for approximately 30 mins until starting to brown. Take the tomato sauce ingredients - crush the garlic clove and blend with all the other sauce ingredients. Season well to taste. Just keep repeating - celeriac, veg, tomato sauce. Finish with a celeriac layer on top. Cover the dish with foil, and place in the oven at 180C. Bake for 30 mins. Drain the cashews and blend all the béchamel ingredients until smooth in a high powered blender such as a Nutri Ninja. Remove the foil from the lasagne and add a generous béchamel layer on top. Sprinkle with dried oregano. You can also add thin tomato slices. Cook for an additional 10-15 mins. Remove from oven and allow the béchamel to set for 10 mins before serving.

RASPBERRY 'CHEESE' CAKE

RASPBERRY 'CHEESE' CAKE

INGREDIENTS

FOR THE BASE:
110g Cashews

(can also use almonds)

Soaking water

100g Desicated coconut

265g Pitted dates

30g Coconut oil (melted)

2.5g Vanilla powder

60g Water

5g Cocoa powder

FOR THE FILLING:

720g Cashews

Soaking water

220g Maple Syrup

100g Lemon Juice

220g Coconut Oil (melted)

90g Water

5g Vanilla Powder

Pinch Sea Salt

110g Raspberries (fresh or frozen)

Soy lecithin – can also sub almond flour

DIRECTIONS

Soak the cashews (or almonds) in the some water for 15 minutes. Drain and discard the water. Add the cashews (or almonds) and all ingredients to a food processor and pulse until a sticky, crumbly mixture is made. Line a 25 cm springform tin with baking paper. Place base mix into the tin and flatten evenly as much as you can. Press down well and smooth using the back of a spoon.

Soak the cashews in hot water for 15 minutes. Drain and discard the water. Add the cashews and all ingredients except the lecithin into a blender and blend until a smooth and viscous liquid has formed. If your blender is low powered, this may take 10 mins or more. Thoroughly stir the lecithin into the liquid, then pour over the base. Leave in the fridge to set, or freeze and leave out for an hour to defrost.

BONUS RECIPE

AÇAI BOWL

ACAI BOWL

INGREDIENTS

- Açai berry
- Mixed summer berries
- Unsweetened almond milk
- 1 scoop of vegan vanilla protein
- Pistachio nuts
- Coconut flakes
- Cacao nibs

DIRECTIONS

Grab all the ingredients and blend them together. After making a uniform mixture, dish it out in a bowl. Top with some crunchy granola, pistachio nuts, cacao nibs, and coconut flakes. Enjoy!

THINGS YOU NEED TO KNOW BEFORE GOING VEGAN

Veganism is the single biggest way to lessen your impact on the planet. Going vegan seems quite easy because of all the facts and knowledge we have about our carbon footprints. The ethical, environmental, and health effects of veganism are beyond doubt. But here are some important points that are to be considered before going vegan.

1. You can switch immediately

It is better to dip a toe first, rather than directly jumping into the pool without knowing its depth. This is a common concept behind things and it is not so very rational when it comes to switching to a vegan diet. It is not deep waters that you need to first check its depth; you have eaten vegetables before in your life, healthy and nutritious items, right? You only now have to do it every day instead of doing it every now and then. Yes, it is that simple. I too immediately switched to a vegan diet without any complications and problems whatsoever and I am doing essentially fine.

At the end of the day, it depends on your body type and the time it would require for you to adjust to this new dietary routine. For some people, they can do it almost right on the spot while others might require some time to adjust to this new routine.

2. No immediate weight loss

Losing weight is one of the most amazing benefits of a vegan diet. But, do all types of vegan diets help you lose weight? Is it an overnight game to lose weight through a vegan diet? That's a big No! Being vegan does not mean you will definitely lose weight. If you are

starting a vegan diet with the intention to reduce your obesity, you must consult a nutritionist or consider a vegan food pyramid. Being vegan, you can still have calorie-rich junk food such as a bag of chips. Eating such vegan food constantly can cause weight gain. Being Vegan does not mean that one will automatically lose weight. The first and foremost tactic to lose weight through a vegan diet is to increase fiber intake. Giving your body a fiber-rich diet means you are already 'cleaning out the pipes.' Consuming whole grains, fresh fruits, vegetables, nuts, lentils, seeds, and plant proteins, your weight loss will be naturally facilitated. There are no insider secrets but a combination of a well-planned balanced and well-nourished vegan diet can lead to considerable weight loss.

3.Budget friendly

It's a false idea that going vegan costs a lot of money. Veganism is pocket-friendly and healthy as well. Meat is one of the most expensive foods and cutting that out would surely save you something. The prices of dairy and eggs are already high, so just by going vegan you are surely not breaking your bank. Raw plant-based products are inexpensive. However, if you are following any specific organic diet then things should be calculated first. If your earnings meet your organic requirements then go ahead! Buying typical staple foods, lentils, and seasonal fruits and vegetables are cost-friendly. Buy your food from local commodities and local farmers working for sustainable agriculture, they will give you healthy fresh fruits in bulk that would surely minimize your budget. Eating healthy does not means that you are eating expensive.

Veganism diets are very accommodating, accessible, and affordable.

4.Negative responses, questions, and unsolicited advice

Food is a personal choice, but standing alone in the crowd being vegan is the most critical thing that trips up most new vegans. Friends, families, colleagues, and associates will all definitely have something to say. It's the most annoying part of the process when you have to justify your own private choice. It's a sensitive time; you are challenging the way you were grown, changing habits, adopting a new lifestyle, and in between all this, you also have to give justifications for it.

One always has two options. Either ignore them or stay quiet and let them watch your transformation, or kill the haters with kindness and delicious vegan food. Treat people with kindness even if they are being jerks. Don't give them lectures, but educate those who question your choice. It's always fun giving them answers and watching a mix of sparkle and dullness in their eyes. Try to change their mind by telling your side of the story and how yummy things are!

5.You can eat processed foods

Don't be afraid to try processed vegan foods. Eating vegan does not mean that there is no place for processed or commercial foods in the vegan lifestyle. There are different plant foods mimicing meat and cheese products that make your transition easy. You can eat anything processed as long as it is vegan such as burgers, ice-cream, frozen fake products, chocolates, and vegan pizzas. But it's obvious that more whole grains and less processed stuff is better.

6.Read food labels

Being a vegan, the most important responsibility on your shoulders is to read the nutrition labels. The composition of any food is a must-consider matter for any vegan. Consider food labels as your new best friends. Every time you do a grocery trip, check every single label. Food labels tell us about the nutritional value, ingredients, nutrients breakdown, and calorie count. Just because a food is not non-vegan does not mean that food item is adequate for a vegan diet.

Many of the preservatives and additives added in veggies or processed foods are derived from animals or non-vegan resources. A food color additive known as Natural Red 4 is derived from the dead bodies of female beetles that are dried and Royal Jelly, which is a secretion obtained from the throat glands of honey bees. There are many other additives that may seem non-vegan but are actually directly or indirectly obtained from animals. For example, Aspic (gelatin alternative but obtained from fish or meat), Vitamin D3 (obtained from fish liver or wool of sheep), Whey and Casein. Moreover, do remember that being labeled as vegan does not mean that the food is highly nutritious. It depends upon its composition and manufacturing process. A substantial amount of research always proves beneficial.

7.Vegan food is not boring

Veganism is falsely accused of being boring, with no snacks, no junk, and no fun. However, this is wrong. Here are some of the favorite, yummysnack foods that are vegan. Some of them would surely shock you!

· Oreo: This is purely vegan and every vegan is going to flex that.
· Swedish fish: A soft and chewy candy that is totally vegan with

no fats.

· Also, vegan donuts, vegan scones, vegan macaroons, vegan tiramisu, vegan croissant, vegan meringue, etc.

· Spicy sweet chili Doritos: World-known snack with sweet spice is vegan.

· Twizzlers: All varieties of this sweet snack are vegan.

· Fritos: Though Bar-B-Q flavored, these snacks are corn made and are vegan.

· Fruit by the Foot: Contains no artificial flavors and is vegan.

· Airheads: An artificially flavored candy, but all varieties are vegan.

There are thousands of snacks, candies, sticks, and spiced chips that are purely vegan. Even you would be shocked to know that most energy drinks are vegan. You can drink them freely.

8.Plants would cover your proteins requirements

Protein is a major concern while going vegan. Protein questions are one of the most asked queries from vegans. Protein is quite essential and necessary for bones, muscle mass, and other metabolic activities of the body and should not go unnoticed but there is nothing to worry about. Plant-based products provide you with all kinds of essential nutrients and these plant-derived proteins are even more beneficial than animal proteins. Eating animal protein in bulk can end you up in trouble - animal protein hazards were mentioned previously.

Just combine lentils, beans, and nuts and there you are with all your complete protein. However, critics call it rabbit food to eat only nuts for protein intake but you don't have to eat it raw always. Drizzle some crushed roasted nuts on your deserts and pasta or add cans of lentils and beans in your chili soup and enjoy! You may also add a protein smoothie as an energy booster.

9. You can still dine out

After eliminating several food groups from of your diet, it may seem a stressful task to eat out at restaurants. Just as veganism is gaining popularity day by day so are the vegan restaurants. You can find a variety of vegan restaurants in London such as Joe and the Juice, Mango Tree, Purezza, Stem & Glory, Farmacy, Mildreds, Wulf &Lamb, and Urban Greens. All of these offer a vegan menu with healthy and nutritious food that is 100% vegan and can help you with your health goals. You can choose from this list based on your taste and liking.

Going vegan does not mean that you have given up eating entirely. Going out for a delicious delightful meal is a fun time and a basic right. A good approach is to search for new vegan restaurants, fast food shops, or a vegan café near your area. Thai, Ethiopian, Japanese, and Indian restaurants are great options to consider for vegan food. VegGuide, Vegetarian Resource group, and The Happy Cow app have different options for vegan restaurants available for you. You just have to take the step and the world is yours.

Don't give up the joy and luxury of eating out. Instead, confidently share your restrictions and requirements with the restaurant staff, and ask them for the best they have. Even if some of the products on your menu appear to be vegan, ask the waiter about the ingredients, telling them your dietary needs to make sure no animal-derived products are added.

10. Can children do a vegan diet?

It is safe for children to go vegan. Plant-based food and vegan diets can provide them with all the essential nutrients needed for their growth and development. Consultation with a nutrient expert may be a good idea. They can provide health charts and diet plans for all age groups ranging from infants to old age individuals. The utilization of supplements and fortified foods would be a necessary part of their diet.

11. Veganism is not a restriction

Veganism is not a restriction or limitation. Think of vegan as a new challenge, a more creative outlet to prove your potential. Consider it an opportunity to experiment with yourself, while moving towards a better good. Veganism is not about cutting your favorites out, it's about discovering a whole new world of delicious flavors, delicate textures, new places, and appetizing dishes. Invite people to your house for dinners, educate them, and introduce to them the exciting option of becoming vegan. Find the vegan and vegan-friendly restaurants. Have fun experimenting with new vegan recipes, consuming various plant-based products and proteins, vibrant and rich nutrient diet, and fiber-packed whole grain. Live, work, travel, enjoy, and stay healthy.

HOW TO GO VEGAN FOR BEGINNERS

Have you stepped towards veganism and faced various challenges? Shifting yourself from a non-vegan to a vegan is a gradual, slow, and continuous process. One can't directly leave meat, milk, and dairy products easily. There are many resources and different ways to approach this. A beginner doesn't even have the idea for starting this transition.

What are you supposed to eat? What is good for providing enough calories and to keep you healthy? To start with the right plant based diet, review your diet plans with your nutritionist. In this way, your body will be tuned gradually according to the new diet plans of vegan foods advised by the nutritionist and you will become a vegan while maintaining your health.
Following essential tips must be followed by beginner vegans for good health.

1. Be ready for it
You have to prepare yourself mentally and physically when you have decided to become a vegan. Collect information about it by doing some research work. What foods should be focused on as a beginner? The pyramid of vegan food is entirely different than that of the conventional pyramid.
Visit your nearby restaurants and local stores. Observe what varieties they are offering in vegan foods and what possible options you have. If you are still confused about products for your vegan

pantry, make a grocery list of healthy vegan foods. After deciding to become a vegan, increase your knowledge about vegan diets and their positive as well as negative impacts on your body health. Discover new techniques of cooking that make these more delicious for you. A number of apps are available to teach and guide you in the best way to prepare a variety of foods. You are welcomed into new exciting journeys, which have a lot of discoveries ahead.

2. Start with the tempo you can manage

Some people think that it's an overnight journey to become a vegan, but it's not like that. It is a slow and gradual transition, as it isn't an easy game to quit and restrict the foods that you have been eating for so long, especially your favorite ones. You have to eliminate red meat in the first week, then remove fish, eggs, and poultry, and so on. One can start it as a challenge for 30 days. It can be overwhelming if you decide to never look back. If you try it for 30 days, it will be easier for you to meet the challenge.

3. Learn vegan diet substitutes

When you are shifting to a vegan diet, you may think that you will never taste eggs or cheese again. It's natural to crave them because you have grown up with these tastes. But if you know about available substitutes, you can get the taste of the cheese or eggs from the plant-based options. Luckily, there are many substitutes for vegan foods with excellent results at an inexpensive price. Necessary ingredients can also replace some foods and still get the required flavors in your vegan foods.

4. Eat simple and diverse meals

Some people overcomplicate things when they are going vegan.

They directly want to use the alternatives of meat, cheese, fish, etc. They make complicated recipes and when they fail, they beat themselves. Just make meals that are simple and diverse. You don't need to focus on complicated cooking and recipes that are time-consuming because you have just decided to choose a vegan diet. You are a beginner to vegans now. You have to focus on eating whole food like grains, fruits, vegetables, legumes, starches, seeds, and nuts. Try to eat different foods so that your body gets a wide range of vitamins, antioxidants, and minerals.

5. Welcome changes in the body and don't panic

As all of us are different, so each of our bodies will react differently to vegan diets when we are transitioning to veganism. In the first two weeks, after making the decision to be vegan, the body may become detoxified. You may get headaches and notice changes in your energy level, but you don't need to be panic about it. The first 3-5 days you might feel muddy and have a slight headache with irritation. Meanwile, you must keep hydrated so the body can detoxify itself. After the detoxification phase passes, people start feeling energetic, have improved mood, cognition, decreased bloating and heaviness after meals, etc. The human body has the best adaption skills but it takes time. Your body will have to pass detox mode if you were used to eating heavy meat in the past. Symptoms vanish after one month so you don't need to worry about it. If anything, if you are worried much about it, talk to your specialist.

6. Adopt the habit of reading the food labels

Some food brands do an excellent job. They put a little title in the label "Suitable for Vegans." This makes it convenient and easy for vegans. Some also draw a special logo for vegans on the label. But unfortunately, some food labels don't have a logo or statement, so you are compelled to read the ingredients very carefully in the list on the label. Some animal ingredients are very difficult to detect. Beware of gelatin, egg white, lactose, and casein because these contain non-vegan

elements and ingredients. For this purpose, download the vegan app. You just have to scan the ingredients list and it tells you whether the food is for vegans or not. You should also be conscious of certain ingredients being used in cosmetics. Use the Bunny free app or Lifesum app which helps you find brands that do testing on animals.

7. Join the community of vegans

If you don't have a vegan friend, your transition phase might be boring and very isolating. You have to follow a vegan friend or mentor during the transition phase if possible. Man is a social animal. Ask questions to your vegan friends, ask them to share their experiences, and get inspired by it. Seek necessary support from them. Start a vegan blog and share your story as well. You can join a community both online and offline because it's very beneficial. You can follow vegans on Instagram and you can join Facebook groups for vegans. If you are finding it difficult to find some vegan friends, start following some vegan accounts on Twitter and Tumblr. There are a lot of recipes on social media for delicious vegan meals as a number of people are transitioning to vegan diets every day. This network is growing in the global village of the internet. Just keep in mind that you are not all alone in this transition journey. A huge community of people will be there for you.

8. Stay Compassionate

You don't have to strive for perfection. Everyone makes mistakes. It might be possible that you purchase a food that contains ingredients derived from animals in it. You may be served bread having butter on top of it (and you don't know about it). For example,"Soy milk" in Thailand contains actual ingredients of cow's milk. So, it is a silly mistake not to bother checking the ingredient list of this milk made by many people

9. Accept Mistakes and Move on

Don't ever give up. Never let your morale down. Don't allow these silly mistakes to interfere with your determined decision of becoming a vegan. We don't live in a vegan world, so if by mistake or unintentionally, you break your vegan streak it does not mean that you have failed. Don't lose hope and always hope for the best. Vegans are also humans and thus are not meant to be perfect every time. Do not beat yourself up; get real motivation and you won't give up. Keep trying for the best.

DIET PLANS AND MENU FOR BEGINNER VEGANS

A vegan diet is a plan for eating in which meat and products derived from animals have to be eliminated from your list. Vegan diets have many benefits like weight loss protection against chronic diseases. Finding a balanced and healthy meal for a vegan diet can be difficult and confusing. If it is planned improperly, vegan diets can cause a deficiency of nutrients and health issues. People decide to become vegans for many reasons like ethical concerns and religious principles. Some decide to decrease their ecological footprint. Some are attracted to veganism for the health benefits.

Following is a healthy plan for vegan meals and a sample menu to start.

· Fresh produce vegetables: bell pepper, cabbage, carrots, garlic, potatoes, tomatoes, spinach, kale flower, kale, asparagus, broccoli, zucchini, etc.

· Fresh produce fruits: apples, blueberries, limes, peaches, pomegranates, bananas, pears, limes, kiwis, strawberries, oranges, grapefruit, etc.

· Frozen produce vegetables: broccoli, carrots, corn, green beans, Brussels sprouts, peas, cauliflower, broccoli and vegetable medley, etc.

· Frozen produce fruits: cherries, mangoes, blueberries, pineapples, blackberries, strawberries, raspberries, etc.

· Whole grains: brown rice, bulgur, oats, farro, quinoa, sorghum, bulgur, teff, buckwheat, barley, sorghum, etc.

· Bread and pastas: wheat pasta, brown rice wraps, sprouted bread (Ezekiel Bread), whole wheat and brown rice pasta, etc.

· Protein sources like nuts: almonds, cashews, peanuts, walnuts, pecans, macadamia nuts, pistachios, hazelnuts, and Brazil nuts

· Protein sources like seeds: Chia seed, hemp seed, sesame seed, sunflower seed, flaxseed, and pumpkin seed

· Protein sources like legumes: Lentils, Black pea, Chickpea, kidney beans, navy beans, pinto beans, etc.

· Protein sources like soy products: tofu, tempeh, etc.

· Protein Powders like powder of peas, powder of brown rice, and hemp protein

· Dairy alternatives/milk substitutes: cashew, flax, almond, oat, rice, coconut, and soy milk

· Yogurt substitutes: cashew, almond, rice, and soy yogurts

· Vegan cheese: parmesan cheese for vegans sliced and shredded varieties, vegan Feta cheese, cheddar cheese, cheese spread, etc.

· Egg alternatives: chia seed, aquafaba, flax meals, arrowroot powder, cornstarch, prepackaged egg substitutes for vegans and silken tofu

· Healthy fats: avocados, coconut oil, unsweetened coconut, flax oil, tahini, and avocado oil

· Snack Foods: dark chocolate, fruit leather, nut butter, popcorn, seaweed crisps, roasted Chickpeas, trail mix, pita chips, dried fruits, edamame, fruit leather, hummus, and nut butter

· Sweeteners: dates, molasses, stevia, monk fruit, maple syrup, and coconut sugar

· Condiments and spices: Chili powder, cumin, ground ginger, cayenne pepper, cinnamon, garlic powder, nutritional yeast, paprika, rosemary, turmeric, thyme, and pepper

SAMPLE OF A VEGAN WEEKLY MEAL PLAN

Here is a sample of the weekly plan for beginners. Easy for beginners to follow because it contains nutritious foods.

MONDAY
Breakfast: Bowl of berries
Lunch: Pasta of whole grain with meatballs of lentil and a side salad
Dinner: Chickpea tacos and cauliflower with guacamole
Snacks: Trail mix and kale chips

TUESDAY

Breakfast: Porridge with almond butter and fruits

Lunch: Baked tofu with red cabbage and Brussels sprouts

Dinner: Mushroom loaf with cauliflower and green beans (Italian)

Snacks: Guacamole with bell peppers and fruit leather

WEDNESDAY

Breakfast: Granola with almond milk

Lunch: Avocados, onions, beans, and tomatoes

Dinner: Swiss chard, mushrooms, and butternut squash

Snacks: Protein shake for vegans, mushrooms, and walnuts

THURSDAY

Breakfast: Protein Smoothie

Lunch: Salad bowl with leafy greens

Dinner: Sun-dried tomatoes, olives, peppers, cucumbers with lentil salad, kale, and parsley

Snacks: Vegan protein (tofu), baked sweet potato, and steamed broccoli. Dessert: Blended frozen berries bowl with a scoop of protein powder with nuts and cacao nibs

FRIDAY

Breakfast: Vegan yogurt and frozen berries

Lunch: Wedges of sweet potato

Dinner: Nutritional yeast with Cheese and mac

Snacks: Homemade granola and chia pudding

SATURDAY

Breakfast: Granola with vegan nutella

Lunch: Ginger-garlic tofu with fried veggies and quinoa

Dinner: Onions, tomatoes, corn, bell peppers, and a salad of beans with black-eyed beans

Snacks: Frozen grapes and almond with celery

SUNDAY

Breakfast: A bowl of berries and almond milk

Lunch: Baked potato and grilled asparagus

Dinner: Brown rice with vegetable paella, onions, bell peppers, tomatoes, and chickpeas

Snacks: Hummus with carrots, fruit salad, and almonds

You can start your breakfast by not eating anything and fasting to help you with cognition and concentration; it means that you skip breakfast entirely.

I will add 5 grams of creatine later in the evening if I am going to plan a late workout in the evening. Different variations can be made for each day depending on your mood and the type of food that you want to eat. Such as I would like to go like this: At lunch time, I prefer a salad bowl with leafy greens. In the evening, a macro balanced meal containing vegan protein (tofu), baked sweet potato, and steamed broccoli.

HOW A VEGAN DIET CAN HELP YOU LOSE WEIGHT, BECOME FIT AND LIVE LONGER

Veganism can help you shed extra pounds from your body. The beauty of vegan weight loss is that you don't have to face hardcore restrictions and malnutrition. Plus, you intake more carbs, which give you instant energy. A vegan diet helps you lose weight in the following ways:

LOSS OF WEIGHT with VEGAN FOODS

Vegans on average are 30 pounds skinnier than meat-eaters. When you eat a vegan diet, you don't engulf those animal products which are inflammation boosting. You fill your bowl with plant-based products that don't contain any inflammation boosting material in it. Instead, it contains a high amount of fiber, has a low quantity of oil, and is cooked plainly. These are the major ways for someone to reduce his body weight.

Vegan Diet Is Trending Nowadays For Sustainable And Healthy Loss In Weight

Many people are adopting vegan diets nowadays because they want a healthy and successful weight loss. Keto diets are difficult to sustain while plant-based food is sustainable, healthy, and it also offers immunity to keep your defense and energy strong against sickness because you are shedding pounds from your body. About 23% of people (consumers) are incorporating vegan foods or plant-based diets into their lives.

As the COVID-19 situation is getting more and more critical, the sale of faux meats that are plant-based is up 35% and overall sales of vegan foods are up 90%. It is growing daily because people want food that helps them lose weight and keeps them healthy. Fortunately, vegan diet plans offer both of these–weight loss plus health immunity. We are finding nothing more natural than taking whole

vegan foods that are low in fats and oils. Reasons for increases in vegan food is twofold right now. One reason is that people are avoiding meat during this phase of COVID-19 and the second is that it helps in the loss of body weight and it also provides immunity. A vegan diet is actually what it sounds like in your mind. Eating tons of fruits, vegetables, legumes, nuts, grains, and seeds is a simple method of reducing almost two pounds each week through a vegan diet, which is considered a healthy rate. The upside of a vegan diet is that it is totally natural.

Fiber Is A Secret Weapon For Vegan Dieters

The more fiber in the food, the more the food is healthy. Eating plant foods with ample fiber helps you reduce weight. Fiber has been given the name "regulator" by those who face difficulty in going to the bathroom. It is in fact the "anti-carb" that helps in weight loss.

Diabetes patients are advised to eat low-carb foods. They are also asked to take fiber because the carbs to fiber ratio has high importance over that of carbs alone. This is the reason that fruits don't increase your fats, although they have a higher amount of carbs than that of vegetables in them. Fiber in the food allows your body to access nutrients that are healthy and keep blood sugar low. It also keeps in check the response of your body's insulin. If the level of blood sugar in the blood is low, the lower the response of insulin, and the signal for your body to store the extra amount of energy as fats.

In this way, it improves insulin sensitivity and prevents diabetes. Although, fat intake in low amounts means low to no amount of fats and minimum oils. It helps your body to mobilize the energy (ready) from where it is stored in the body. You use your body glycogen first. Vegan foods that have a low amount of oil are a natural source to burn the stored fats of the body at a faster rate because it prompts the body to take energy from within.

Stay Healthy Because You Are Losing Body Weight By Immune-Boosting Fruits and Vegetables

A vegan dietary plan that contains fruits and vegetables offers your body immune-boosting properties. For all the diets that are known for boosting the natural immunity of the body, the vegan diet is on the top of the list. Mushrooms, peppers, and broccoli are among those thirteen foods that provide natural immunity. A vegan diet helps you lose weight because you eat processed foods in very low amounts. They may have high amounts of sugar, fat, additives, and they contain less fiber. The basic idea for a vegan diet is to allow 20% to 25% of needed calories to come from proteins that are plant-based, 55% to 60% from carbs, and 15% to 25% from fats.

Improved Digestibility And Gut Health

Scientists found that eating a plant-based diet changes the microbiome of the body. A vegan diet increases the healthy bacteria in the digestive system. This improves digestibility, gut health, and prevents diseases like diabetes.

Vegans have a type of gut bacteria known as Bacteroidetes, says

Kahleova's team (participants of a vegan diet). These bacteria digest fiber into short-chain fatty acids, thus improving metabolism.

Tips for Reducing Weight and Belly Fat From Vegan Foods

· Weigh nutrient density versus calories

· Focus on foods with a high amount of fiber. Constant hunger can be one of the reasons for the failure of diets.

· Try carbs instead of fats

· Read the label for the ingredients list

· Avoid processed foods

· Train taste buds with this new vegan taste

· Keep your food in the fridge

· Avoid inflammation boosting foods that are mostly animal or derived from animals

· Hang out with health-focused friends

One of the reasons for reducing weight after adopting veganism is that people stop consuming dairy products that contain a high amount of fats and calories. Beyond that, many people eat dairy products in all meals and even in snacking also. The result is that they become obese. It is said that obesity is the mother of diseases. A vegan has a very low risk of diseases caused by obesity and excess fats. If a vegan does not feel the scale moving towards a weight decrease, it can be because of two reasons. It is possible that he is still cooking and eating food with oil. The second is that he is eating too much (too many calories). Research shows that vegans lose more weight compared to non-vegans because they don't eat meat. Plant-based diets of vegetables and fruits contain a low amount of calories and a high amount of nutrients. These are also an important part of the diet that is heart-healthy.

A study from Harvard University in 2016 revealed that vegan dieters lost much more weight than non-vegans over an 18-week period. Avocados, bananas, berries, yogurt, skim milk (chocolate), citrus, and green tea help in the burning of belly fat. Leafy vegetables like kale, spinach, and lettuce help you burn belly fats very quickly. You can reduce your tummy if you adopt veganism. In short, vegan diets or veganism is the best way for someone to lose bodyweight and extra fat from the belly and the whole body.

A VEGAN DIET HELPS YOU IN IMPROVE YOUR FITNESS

A very common misconception we still hear about vegans is that they can't be as fit as a person who takes proteins from dairy products and meat. This concept is not true at all. There is nothing about vegan food that makes you sluggish. Modern research, experiments, studies, and observations show that a vegan diet is far better than a non-vegan diet because it keeps you more fit and active. Vegan diets conform to fitness and health. Vegan diets improve their performance.

Following are the benefits which vegan foods offer for your fitness.

· Staples of vegans like grains and legumes make you feel fuller, less sluggish, and lighter because they provide natural energy.

· Plant-based foods contain a higher amount of antioxidants, which assist in the restoration of muscles after a hard work out.

· Proteins that are derived from vegan diets are non-acidic while proteins obtained from meat are acidic in nature and have negative effects on the density of bones and calcium.

· You will have more stable energy by eating plant-based diets.

· A vegan feels less droopy and bloated after eating a meal while non-vegan foods make you slow and sleepy after a meal.

· A vegan has a lower risk of nausea and cramps because his food is digested easily.

· A vegan's hormones are more balanced, which keeps him always fit.

· A vegan lifestyle helps you improve your performance and stamina.

· Switching to veganism benefits your body with less swelling of joints, more energy production, weight loss, and high endurance.

A common mistake that most people make to become fit is that they take large amounts of salads and vegetables, which are stomach filling and healthy, but don't provide enough calories to keep you fit. It's important to include carbohydrates like potatoes and cooked grains or proteins like nuts or beans with salads and vegetables to become active, sharp, and fit.

Some important nutrients to keep your body energetic and fit include:

· Iron is found in pistachios, nuts, spinach, and resins.

· Calcium from greens like kale, Brussels sprouts, and broccoli are rich with calcium. It supports and strengthens your body and bones which keep you fit.

· Vitamin C, Vitamin D, Vitamin B-12, Amino acids, and Omega-3 can be found in cereals, soya beans, and various vegetables.

· Proteins can be found from many resources like lentils, quinoa, beans, nuts, seeds, and tofu.

Take plenty of water, sleep, rest, and get sunlight for Vitamin D. As vegans eat legumes, seeds, beans, nuts, green veggies, fruits, whole grains, supplements, or soy milk, they are always fit, energetic, and active because these diets are highly nutritious, easily digestible, and remove excess fats from the body. A study based on 15,000 American vegetarians compared them to those who are meat-eaters and found that the non-vegetarians are at twice the risk of being on blood pressure drugs, aspirin, laxatives, painkillers, insulin, tranquilizers, and sleeping pills.

VEGAN DIETS HELP YOU LIVE LONGER

Do vegans live a longer life??? Is that true???
The sweet and simple answer to this question is YES. On average, vegans live a longer life. They are expected to have a longer life as compared to meat-eaters because they get old with no health issues. But why is that?
Before we dive into the science and evidence of plant-based foods, an important point must be kept in view. Some meat-eaters are healthy and some are unhealthy. The same is the case for vegans. Some vegans are healthy and some are unhealthy. But according to modern research, vegetarians and vegans live a longer life. Vegan diets tend to:
· Lower blood pressure
· Lower risk of heart diseases
· Lower risk of cancer incidence (overall)
· Less chance for becoming a diabetic patient
· Lower risk of getting all those diseases that have a high mortality rate
· Reduced number of pathogenic bacteria (gut) and high abundance of protective species.

Vegans don't eat meat: All meat including the white meat of a
chicken has high cholesterol
and saturated fatty acids
which are highly associated
with cardiac diseases. Eggs
and dairy also have a high
amount of saturated fats.
Processed meat such as
salami, bacon, ham,
sausage, canned and smoked

meat is classified as a carcinogen of Class-1 by WHO (World Health
Organization). It shows that the evidence is as strong as that of
asbestos and smoking. All red meat including beef, goat, pork and
lamb, etc. are also classified as Class-2 carcinogens. It means that
they are obviously cancer-causing. Livestock is given antibiotics
and hormones to increase their body weight and milk production.
Hence, dairy and meat contain these antibiotics and hormones,
which have very negative impacts on human health. As vegans don't
eat these saturated fatty acids resources, foods, and carcinogens,
they don't develop these high mortality diseases. Vegans eat more
healthy foods. This is by default because when you don't eat meat
and dairy products, you have to eat alternatives to these. It is also
noted that vegans concentrate more on their health.

A person who is more conscious about his health mostly adopts
veganism. Vegetables and fruits contain bioactive compounds that
are protective like polyphenols, antioxidants, vitamins, minerals,
and fibers. These work through mechanisms to reduce the oxidative
stress, lower blood level (VLDL), and also cholesterol (LDL).
Whole grains contain phytochemicals, antioxidants, vitamins,
minerals, and protein. As they are highly nutritious, they also reduce

the risk of heart disease, lower blood sugar, reduce body weight, less risk of becoming diabetic and reduced risk of cancer. So, one can reduce his body weight, improve his fitness, and in fact, he can increase his lifespan by avoiding the animal-based and animal derived products (meat and dairy) and adopting a plant-based diet (veganism).

Nearly a decade more of life–that's what you get when you switch from animal-based eating to plant-based dietary pattern. Vegans live up to 15 years longer than non-vegans and it's considered the same life spending gap that is expected between smokers and non-smokers.

SURVEY ON VEGAN LONGEVITY

Research was carried out at Massachusetts General Hospital in which they analyzed the diet and health of 130,000 people for a time span of thirty years. They detected that every three percent increase in calories from plant-based protein lessened the risk of death by 10 percent. This number rises to 12 percent for the threat of dying from heart disease.

Heart disease is the leading cause of death in the world. Dr. Dean Ornish, almost 20 years ago, said that heart disease cannot be stopped but it can be reversed by a vegan diet. Dr. Ornish's team demonstrated that the blood of vegan men had 8 times the cancer combating power, and women can enhance their ability to fight off breast cancer by taking only two weeks of plant-based diet.

Alzheimer's disease is marked as the sixth leading killer. Meat eaters are likely to dement three times more than those who are vegan. New research shows that eating plant-based foods like spice saffron worked well as an Alzheimer's drug.

"Our overall findings support significant sources of plant-based protein for long-term health," says Dr. Mingyang Song, a lead scientist.

As vegans don't eat these all-saturated fatty acids resourced foods, they don't develop these high mortality diseases.

FASTING ON A VEGAN DIET

Fasting is when you willfully refrain from eating. It is quite common practice in different cultures and religions to promote health, longevity, and fulfill religious customs. There can be countless reasons for fasting but nowadays fasting is used as a tool for weight loss and betterment of the body's health. The combination of veganism and fasting has been proven to enhance the metabolic activities of the body, from increasing the energy level to maintain body weight and mental health. But most importantly, limiting your calories for a long period can be scary, dangerous, simply not fun, and this shouldn't happen at any cost.

There is always a right and wrong way. So it's very important to coach yourself on what, why, and how to fast. That's where intermittent fasting with a plant-based diet comes. When you get a combination of intermittent fasting and a plant-based diet you get twice the benefits of losing weight and disease prevention.

Fasting along with a vegan diet might restrict your nutrients, so a well-planned diet is necessary. Vegan fasting is a dietary pattern in which there are certain periods of fasting and eating. It means that for a specific period you will fast and then open your feast window for a certain period.

Fasting Protocols

There are several different approaches to explain how to fast. It's incredibly important to choose the right method of fasting. Take a look at the following protocols to combine with a vegan diet and choose the best method for your fasting plan.

· **5:2**: For 5 days of the week, eat normally as per your routine. For the next two days of the week, take 500-600 kcals. 500 kcal are recommended for women and 600 kcal for men.

· **16:8**: Fast for 16 hours of the day and open your feast window of the day for 8 hours. This is the most common one. You can start with 12 hours fast and slowly get in tune with your 16 hours fast.

· **Eat-stop-eat**: This point refers to a fast of 24 hours for 1 to 2 times a week. You don't eat anything for 24 hours. An example is not eating from lunch of one day to the lunch of the next day.

· **Alternate fasting day**: Eat very low calories about 500 kcal every other day, and eat normally on alternate days.

None of these methods ask you to fast for two days, and also, the intake of calories is enough. Stick to any of these four methods and you will not go wrong. However, your choice depends on your needs and preferences.

How to Fast For The 16:8 Fasting Method

1. Omit your breakfast.

2. Do not eat anything until lunchtime or at least up to 10 am or 11 am in the morning.

3. Complete your dinner by 6 pm or 7 pm.

4. Repeat the same routine the next day.

What to eat in vegan fasting

During fasting, you eat nothing. Before you begin your fast days, design a diet plan. Fruits and simple plant-based diets digest faster than meat so eat the foods that take some longer time to digest during your fasting time.

· Whole grains, nuts, and beans are the best options to consider, as they take more time to digest. They help your stomach to stay full longer.

· Look over your diet and calculate vitamins and minerals intake. Make sure you are getting every nutrient in a balanced amount.

· Supplements can help maintain the level of minerals and nutrients.

· During fasting, you cannot intake any calories but can consume liquid with no calories.

· Drink plenty of water. Vegan meals have high water content but when you are fasting you have to replenish that loss by drinking water. Drink up to 10 cups of water while you are fasting.

· Break the fast with some light foods like fruits, smoothies, or salads. Do not start with nuts as it's heavy to digest. Leave it for the main course.

Best Foods to Keep the Stomach Full While Fasting

Successful vegan fasting depends upon a healthy diet. It's important to keep your stomach full for a longer time. Fill your stomach with balanced, nutritional, and stomach-filling foods. Filling foods refer to those food items that are rich in fiber, proteins, and water but have low density.

Whole grains: Incorporating a bowl full of whole grains can greatly help you to keep full for a long time. Whole grains digest slowly. Some whole grain recipes include roasted beet sorghum salad, oatmeal, porridge, kale furrow, and mushroom bowl.

Starchy vegetables: These vegetables are more robust and heavier.

Pumpkin, white potatoes, carrots, corns, sweet potatoes, and beets contain a higher level of carbohydrates that provide you energy for a long time but do not overuse them. Some recipes using starchy vegetables are Quinoa curry, Vegan Butternut squash, kale, and potato casserole.

Seeds and nuts: They are the heartier snacks of any meal. These tummy fillers are packed with fiber, unsaturated fats, and proteins. Drizzle or sprinkle the nuts as toppings on your every meal, while seeds give you nutrients, flavor, and aroma. Try diverse recipes using seeds and nuts such as baked cashew nuts, weed green smoothie, vegan cookies with almonds, pasta with tomato sauce, and pumpkin sauce.

Legumes: Legumes are typical vegan foods. High in proteins, packed with fiber, and low in calories. Legumes are a staple of vegans. Lentils belong to the legume food group and is an essential part of every vegan kitchen. Legumes feature recipes that include red lentil burgers, chili lime tacos, chickpea spinach with lentils, boiled rice with lentils, and red lentils curry.

How to begin vegan fasting

The best way to do something is to begin. The beginning of anything pops up several questions; however, it is not too perplexing in the case of vegan fasting. It's easier than it looks if you are educated and smart to make a start.

Make a plan

Fasting requires a well-managed and planned diet as there may be hard times if you start on your own without any specific diet plan. There are many ways to set your boundaries and choose a diet protocol. Go with your instincts while choosing a protocol. Do not take it for granted as taking only 500 calories and then fasting 16 hours to 24 hours will not work for you. Best to not follow other people's advice and experiences. Go with the one that is more sustainable and suits your body.

Ease into it

It is said that slow and steady wins the race. Don't try to become a rabbit and run directly to your goal. Give yourself some time to ease into the process. If you have selected 16 hours of fasting for yourself, it would be difficult for you to sustain it all at once. There are chances that you may trip off your goals and get fed up. Start with a 5-hour fast then move to 8 and 10 hours fasting, it will help your body to get into the habit of fasting. Ease into the process for long-lasting results.

Set a target time

Everything takes time to show its effectiveness. After choosing a plan, set a review time of 30 days or 40 days. Give it a good try and analyze its efficacy. If it does not work for you, do not get upset and don't give up the idea of fasting, try another diet protocol. Experiment with different fasting methods and you will surely find your best one.

Plan to succeed

Fasten your belt before the race begins. We usually make better healthy choices when we plan in advance. This is significant when you are fasting because once your fasting period is over and your feast window opens you will eat anything available in a hurry. In this haste, eating junk is not adequate. Instead, one should focus on healthy fiber-rich foods that will prove sustainable while fasting.

Benefits of vegan fasting

Fasting performed in a safe and healthy manner ends up giving you a lot of advantages. Fasting done in a planned way is worth the work. Some of the major benefits of vegan fasting are mentioned below:

Weight loss

Obesity and weight loss are a billion-dollar empire. Everyone is looking to reduce unwanted pounds in the fastest way. Rapid vegan weight loss is feasible with fasting and a healthy diet. The popularity of vegan fasting is basically because of the health and weight management it provides. Firstly, fasting controls your hunger. The desire to eat food is still present in your gut but you refrain from eating. The bad habits of eating in excess should soon vanish. Secondly, a major biological reason for weight loss is the lower level of insulin in vegan fasters. Lower insulin enables the body to burn fat instead of glucose and thus aids to combat obesity and helps in weight management. Fasting helps you reduce weight by removing extra fat and muscle mass.

If you remain consistent, a loss of 1lb to 2lbs per week can be observed. You can maintain your "Happy weight" by vegan fasting.

Aging and longevity

Vegan fasting tends to increase life years and your age with agility. Several experiments have been done to know about the connection between longevity and fasting. Restricting calories extends the life span.

Clive McCay of Cornell University in 1930 discovered that rats who were subjected to dieting at an early age were at less risk to develop cancer and other diseases in their old age. Moreover, fasting leads to increased autophagy. Autophagy is the self-destruction or death of cells and regeneration. During fasting, this process increases and there is more removal of debris and biological waste from the body. New cells are formed which is an asset to aging with grace.

Increased Endurance

Vegan fasting has proved to enhance physical strength. There are several factors in vegan fasting that lead to an increase in the endurance of the body. One of the main factors is the glycogen molecule. Glycogen molecules are essential to maintain blood glucose level by storing the glucose molecule. Depletion of glycogen takes 10 to 12 hours during which fats from the tissues are released, they are then converted into ketone bodies and are transferred to the tissues to be used as energy. Thus, eating within a period of 8 to 9 hours and fasting for 15 to 16 hours enhances endurance. Vegan fasting improves mitochondrial biogenesis, meaning more mitochondrial cell production and thus more energy.

Improves mood

During the initial weeks, you may feel irritated or deal with some anger issues. In the long run, vegan fasting improves your focus and mood. Vegan fasting increases the production of a protein known as BDNF. This protein in the brain connects to improved mood by 50% to 100%. Moreover, vegan fasting can be helpful in treating depression.

Prevent diseases

As dieters eat healthy food and adopt a better lifestyle of fasting, they have the ability to combat threatening diseases. Vegan fasting reduces the risk of diabetes, heart disease, and different types of cancer.

It also reduces the risk of inflammation, reduces acne, improves insulin sensitivity, reduces bad cholesterol, and maintains glucose levels.

Why and who should try vegan fasting?

Vegan fasting can be considered important as it carries many benefits. Fasting with a plant-based diet is the right path for you. It's simple. Vegan fasting does not require any additional supplements, diet plans, meal planning, or exercise routines. It will also reduce the cost of food. Vegan fasting is that much more effective as restricting calories from your diet. Everything is not meant for everybody. Before jumping into the deep end, one should first analyze their circumstances, health, and position.

The following people should consider vegan fasting:

1. Vegans who want to reduce weight: Fast weight loss is possible with vegan fasting, it makes it easier for you to get your body toned and reduce obesity. Try vegan fasting and get the body you desire.
2. Vegans who want to improve their workout: Survey reveals that vegan fasting boost growth hormones and enhance metabolic functions as much as 500%, making it easier to perform better at the gym.
3. Vegans who want to eradicate bad eating habits: A few vegans eat unhealthy and junk vegan food unintentionally. Plant-based fasting will help you adopt healthy and good eating habits.

What Happens To Your Body In the Fasting State?

Your blood sugar is rising right after you have a meal. The carbohydrates are being processed as glucose and released into the blood stream. This causes insulin production. The action of insulin is storing energy and absorption of blood sugar. This takes up to 3 hours. After that the glucose is being transported to our blood and tissues and the energy from the fat is not used as a primary source of energy.

However, after 9 hours of fasting, the food is been disimilated and the body stops producing insulin. The blood sugar drops, however the hormone glucagon is been released into the blood stream and the energy supply remains constant. After 11 hours of fasting, the body starts producing fat burning hormones. These hormones perform fat metabolism: Human growth hormone HGH, Insulin growth factor IGF, Glucagon, testosterone, adrenaline, and Triiodothyronine T3. After 12-16 hours, ketosis begins. Ketones are produced in the liver as a by-product of fat metabolism. Their function is to produce energy to the heart and vital organs. Ketones are known for nerve cell activation, helping with concentration, and intellectual capacity keeping you productive. A process called autophagy starts between 14-18h after a meal. This is described as cells recycling themselves. They not only recycle but also renew, which you can guess about the benefits there.

Top tip: I would probably not recommend fasting for longer than 16 hours as it might lead to burn out.

Who should not try vegan fasting?

The following people should not consider the idea of following vegan fasting dietary patterns:

1. Vegans who are pregnant or breastfeeding: If you are a vegan who

is pregnant or breastfeeding then you ought not to experiment with different fasting proposals. Your baby's nourishment relies upon you and you should be careful in those days.

2. Vegans who are diabetic: Though vegan fasting helps with diabetes, it is not recommended for diabetic vegans to select fasting proposals and go on fasting on their own. It might disturb their sugar level.

TIPS TO EAT VEGAN AT RESTAURANTS AND HOW TO CONVINCE YOUR FAMILY/FRIENDS TO BECOME VEGAN

If you are a vegan and you are going out with your friends and family then it should not pose any problem whatsoever. Everyone can enjoy a meal regardless of what they want to eat and what they don't. There should not be any emphasis from one group to another for trying out their specific menu or diet. This type of culture is already getting hit in the UK and various European destinations such as Spain and Greece where Russian people are also well aware of the vegan style of dining and cooking. A good understanding of the vegan diet is already taking over multiple restaurants, which are now serving extensive and specially crafted vegan menus just to accommodate their vegan patrons along with the other food groups. There is good news for vegans. Restaurants are becoming conscious of allergies and dietary restrictions. They are offering new options on menus for vegans. The more demand for something, the more it will change in the future. Vegans are looking forward to the day when vegan options on the menu will be normal rather than uncommon or scarce.

The following few tricks and tips are helpful for vegans when they are out in a restaurant.

1. Check the Menu of the Restaurant Online and Plan Ahead

Obviously, it's not possible to eat vegan diets everywhere. It may be a friends' birthday or a family gathering. Before visiting any restaurant, check the menu of the restaurant online to check for vegan items. Hopefully, you will find some vegan items on the menu for you. But unfortunately, some restaurants don't have any ingredients for vegans on their menu. If there are some dishes for vegetarians, you can ask them to modify these for you like removing chicken. Keep note of all these dishes before going to the restaurant so that you can simply order there without much wasting of time and pondering over the selection of vegan dishes.

2. Contact the restaurant for vegan options and menus

If you don't find any obvious vegan meal options on the menu, make a phone call to the restaurant and ask them if they can accommodate any vegan meal for you. Tell them your dietary restrictions and ask if they can accommodate your choice in accordance with their policies.

Don't feel any pain or embarrassment because it's your lifestyle and that's the way you eat. You will receive your fair share of enthusiasm in such a way, "Yes sir! We can make anything for you that you want." You will find that the chef of the restaurant thinks that a plate of vegetables is a satisfying vegan dinner. For example, if you want to eat a tofu stir fry or a pizza, don't be afraid to ask them, "Can you make it for me following vegan diets?" Most restaurants consider customers as their priority, so hopefully you would be served well.

Some restaurants also have secret menus!! For example, a restaurant named PARADISO in Oakville has a vegan menu. But guess what?? They don't display their vegan menu to the customer until he or she asks them for it. Horrors… This menu has several delicious dishes and vegan options. You will feel blessed to see it. You will realize that it's not normal for restaurants to have separate menus. But it's not abnormal to ask them for a vegan menu and let them know that you are a vegan.

3. Get creative for substitutes

When you are a vegan then it's perfectly okay to ask for some alterations in food. Some vegetarian items can be made vegan in a simple way by just altering the butter with oil or leaving the cheese off. If your options are limited, ask them if they can make these swaps for you. Order some side items (asking them to not use butter) to make your meal. Instead of cheese toppings on salad, ask for some avocado or nuts. Ask for substitutions and make sure you get the food you want.

4. Order sides

Make sides your best friend when dining in a non-vegan restaurant. Sides are always safe to order and you already know what you are going to have. Order many sides and make your own meal. Different restaurants have varied side options, such as fried potatoes, fried veggies, baked sweet potatoes, rice with sauce, and many others. If you are not in a veggie mood, order some gingerbread or fruit bread with a hot beverage and enjoy.

5. Eat beforehand if options are limited severely

When you have done your research and feel that the options there will be limited severely, eat a little meal beforehand. During family time in the restaurant have some coffee, tea, or an herb drink with a salad. It ensures that you will not feel deprived at the restaurant with friends or family, and it's not a big deal if you are determined.

6. Take a fun Beverage

If you are a vegan and want all parts of your diet to depict the same then it is recommended that you try out the non-alcoholic beverages specially crafted for vegans such as Kombucha. You will become a fan of this amazing non-alcoholic fermented tea. It has the same color as champagne minus the alcoholic nature. The vegan oriented purpose behind this drink is that it is exceptionally healthy such as it has amazing gut health benefits due to the high amount of probiotics present in this amazing tea.

7. Eat vegan apps

If you are vegan then you would be very grateful to these Eat Vegan apps like Happy Cow and Vegman. Happy Cow is one of the most popular vegan apps. Searching for vegan-friendly restaurants on the Happy Cow website in the nearby area when you are out or traveling is the best tip for vegans. It's quite simple. You type your location and find all vegan-friendly restaurants listed on your smart device in the nearby area. These types of apps give you all kinds of necessary information such as menu, contact, address, and reviews. You can also look for new options in your area by asking on Facebook and joining Facebook groups for vegans. Facebook is very helpful because there are ratings and reviews. You can have an idea from the feedback given by others. Many people also tell about the dish which the restaurant's chef prepared for them on the spot and which dish he modified for him.

8. Online review or Comment Card

Restaurants take feedback on comment cards, but it was more common a few years ago. Nowadays, online reviews for any restaurant matters a lot. Online reviews and comment cards let your voice be heard. These are great ways to ask for more vegan options. Mostly, the restaurant owners take note when they read these comments and requests.

9. Don't sweat it

Generally, expectations of a vegan are lower when he thinks about dining out in a restaurant. You focus on your goal and think that it's not a big deal to deal with it. Just be kind and flexible in your behavior. While asking for vegan menus don't get nervous and always talk friendly. Cheers to you! Happy Eating!

10. Seek out the Cuisines which are ethnic

Many cuisines offer natural vegan options that can be modified easily. Vegans love to dine at Mexican, Indian, and Thai restaurants due to the many options they offer for vegans. Some dishes can be made easily with vegan cream without much change in the flavor. Here are some of the dishes that are must-try for a vegan while visiting these restaurants:

· American burger restaurants: You can still fill your stomach at American burger places without having a hotdog and hamburger. Fortunately, now veggie burgers are available at most of these places. You can have black bean burgers, pizza without cheese, wraps, veggie sandwiches, beet burgers, and sweet potato fries.

· Japanese restaurants: You will have a lot of options in Japanese foods such as mushroom and tofu potstickers, a famous Japanese vegan dish and an excellent source of protein for vegans. Moreover, you can also eat Japanese rice balls with sweet potatoes, Udon noodle soup, and Japanese edamame.

· Italian restaurants: Eating at an Italian restaurant can be a bit tricky,

just make sure to ask if there are any hidden eggs or dairy in it. You can look for veggie pizza without cheese, gingerbread, and veggie pasta and bread with olive oil.

· Mexican restaurant: Mexican foods are full of cheese and meat and thus it may sound difficult to eat at Mexican places. However, it's not that tough. Just ask for no cheese and more veggies. You can enjoy veggie tacos, beans and rice, nachos with no cheese, chips with salsa, and sour cream.

· Middle Eastern restaurants: Middle-eastern theme restaurants can give you tons of options for plant and veggie foods. Just ask them not to use butter in your food. Go for mixed fried veggies, spiced chickpea,

lentils with rice, and eggplant with chili in olive oil.

How to convince your Family and Friends to become Vegan

Veganism is increasing day by day. More and more people are adopting it. As it has many benefits for your health and keeps you fit, one should adopt it. It's very rare for a vegan to belongs to a family in which all the members of the family are vegans too. Veganism is adopted slowly and gradually by people after great research and observing its positive effects on nearby vegans. The same is the case with the friends. In most cases, friends are also non-vegans.

It's an ethical duty for the vegan to convince his friends and family to become vegans too so that they also get the benefits from the positive impacts of veganism on the body. Vegans must educate the masses about going vegan as only a vegan knows that it is a great way to live a healthy and cruelty-free life.

Following are some tips and ways for a vegan to persuade his family and friends towards veganism.
· Don't give vegan lectures all day and night; try to convince others by logistics, scientific research, and practical results. Also, one sales pitch is not going to work for everyone, as every person has different concerns and approaches about food, animals, and veganism.

· Be honest about why you adopted veganism. It may sound obvious to someone but a vegan knows that it is the thing you have struggled for the most. You were very proud of yourself and confident about your decision so that you are at this stage. But it is hesitant for a vegan to share it with others because he is afraid of their negative response. You can be very truthful and honest with them. It helps you focus on your beliefs and you can say simply, "Animals should not be harmed by anyone" or "I read an article which revealed
the truth with me about the dairy industry and its products."
Remind them that once you were also in the same position in which the addressed person is right now. It will help them to think about it. They will think that if you can change your mind from being meat-eaters to being vegans, they can also. And the evidence will be standing in front of them with benefits.

· Be Compassionate. Becoming a vegan is all about your compassion. It should be a breeze. The response of some people to logic and hard facts is instant but it is not the same for everyone. Some people take time to make a decision. They may take a long time to adopt veganism and to understand the arguments about it. In our society, it is considered normal and okay to utilize animals and their products. Such ingrained messages don't disappear overnight. After repeated exposure to arguments, people accept it and apply it to their lives. It may be frustrating for you, but you have to accept that your friends and family members will not adopt veganism immediately. They are convinced to adopt veganism at one time and may change their decision at the second. You make the best positive impact on them so that they are impressed and come back. Be a good example of veganism for those who are thinking about it.

· Give them information. Lack of knowledge and information may be the reasons for people not to adopt it. They don't know about the truths of the animal industries and their products. They may be surprised after listening. You are the person who will reveal this truth and share this information with them so that they can make the right decision. Make them aware of the horrors and brutality of factory farming where every year almost 70 billion mammals and 3 trillion sea animals are slaughtered to fill the meat desires of humans. Share the statistics and facts that affected you the most during your vegan journey.
Refer those videos to your friends that helped you. Recommend those eye-opening documentaries. Share easily approachable and accessible products with them. Share vegan recipes that are very simple. It can be a great idea to join a vegan event with your friends and family members so they are highly inspired and get motivated.

When you introduce them to a vibrant community of vegans, they will be excited that they can also be a part of it. Many people attending these vegan events are not actually vegans. They are just curious about it. It will help them to feel right when at home. They will return with all the necessary information.

· Share your Vegan Pledge. Encourage your family members and friends to make a promise for 30 days that they will avoid all non-vegan foods. This pledge helps 80% of the people in successfully adopting veganism. Daily emails are, "Which plant milk should be used in coffee where to buy it." Sharing content from Facebook and Twitter pages may also be a good idea. It demonstrates how simple and fun it is to become a vegan.

· Promote the Vegan Movement. Promoting veganism should be a big part of your life. It's a very good feeling to hear that your friends, parents, siblings, and cousins are also announcing their change to veganism. It is possible if you play a part in making them make such a decision. It reminds you that you are instrumental in the flourishing of the vegan movement. It might possible that you have philosophical debates with your family members and friends about the rights of animals and ethics. Anything that persuades someone to veganism and opens his eyes about its benefits is best.

· Tell them about the benefits. Win over their hearts, showing the vegan health angle. You can persuade or convince your friends by revealing the benefits of veganism with them in detail, one by one. Prove its advantages to them by healthy debate. Tell them that a vegan is more energetic, active, fit, sharp, smart, and talented as compared to non-vegans. He has high endurance if he is an athlete.

Many international elite athletes are vegan and have won many Olympic medals. As a vegan diet is highly nutritious and balanced, vegans live a healthy and sound life. Vegan diets burn extra belly fat and help in reducing weight. Vegans are more fit than non-vegans because they grow old with little health issues and are expected to live a longer life. This can be the most attractive point for non-vegans to adopt veganism.

STUDIES BASED ON A VEGAN DIET

The concept of veganism is now being accepted across the globe. More and more people are adopting a vegan style of living because veganism has many biometric and environmental outcomes. Due to its popularity, scientists are also quite interested in veganism. Thousands of studies and surveys have been done on a vegan diet. As a rough estimate, 7 out of 10 studies based on a vegan diet lean in favor of veganism.

Veganism claim to offer many health benefits, thus collecting randomized data and analyzing it gives more strong shreds of evidence that veganism is pro. The noise on social media about veganism makes people wonder about its scientific basis.

Following are some important studies that make you understand the eminence of veganism:

· American Journal of Clinical Nutrition: A study in 2008 of 21,337 people found that people eating seven or more eggs in a week have a 23% higher mortality rate and those who are diabetics consuming the same amount are at 201% more risk of dying as compared to those who eat less than 1 egg/week.

· Journal of American Heart Association 2019: An article published on August 7, 2019, by the American Heart Association claims that plant-based diets are at less risk of resulting in cardiovascular disease, mortality due to cardiovascular disease, and all-cause mortality in the population of general middle-aged adults.

This study analyzed 12,168 people for a period of 25 years. The results showed that people revolving more around plant-based diets were at less risk of heart diseases, cardiovascular mortality, and all-cause mortality than people consuming more meat. A plant-based diet lessened the incidence of cardiovascular diseases by 16%, reduced the incidence of cardiovascular death by 32%, and decreased all causes of death risk by 18%.

· Elizabeth Blackburn, Noble Prize winner: Research done by Blackburn found that vegan diets result in a change of 500 genes in three months. Vegan diets turn on the genes that prevent heart diseases and turn off the genes that may cause heart disease, any cancer, and other illness.

· The American Journal of Medicine 2005: Effects of a plant-based diet on body weight, metabolism, and insulin sensitivity:

Barnard. N.D.ET AL. studied the effects of low fat and plant-based dietary intervention. Sixty-four overweight women were selected for this experiment. Each woman was randomly given a low-fat vegan or a low-fat control diet plan. This low-fat control diet plan was based on the National Cholesterol Education Program. These women followed the diet plans for 14 weeks.

After analysis, results showed that vegans ingested less protein, fats, cholesterol, and more fiber than the NCEP control diet group.

Participants following the vegan diet plan lost a mean weight of 5.8 kg (12.8lbs) as compared to the NCEP diet group who lose an average of 3.8 kg (8.4lbs). The vegan group showed more changes in BMI and waist circumference. Metabolism and insulin sensitivity was also significantly improved.

· The Journal of Pediatrics, 2015: Impact of Plant-based, non-fat diet or American Heart Association diet on obese children and their parents having hypercholesterolemia and probability of cardiovascular disease.

This analysis was done by Mackin, M. E AL. in 2015. For this study, thirty obese children and their parents were enlisted. Each pair was randomly allocated to follow a vegan plant-based diet or an American Heart Association diet (AHA diet) for a period of 4 weeks. As per the results, a significant decrease was seen in the total calories of both groups. Parents and children who were following a vegan diet consumed less Vitamin D, cholesterol, saturated fats, protein, and Vitamin B12 as compared to the American Heart Association diet group.

However, more carb and fiber intake was shown by the vegan diets. During the four-week period, obese children consuming a vegan diet showed a weight loss of 3.1 kg (6.7lbs). This weight loss was 197% more than those who were following the American Heart Association diet.

The vegan group children showed a minimization in systolic blood pressure, LDL cholesterol level, and total cholesterol level, while the American Heart Association diet group didn't show any change. Parents consuming vegan food had approximately 0.16% lower levels of A1C hemoglobin; these levels are a measure of blood sugar control, lower total cholesterol levels, and lower LDL levels. Vegan parents lost 1.6kg (3.5lbs) more than parents of the American Heart Association diet. Both diets reduced the risk of heart disease in children and adults. However, a vegan diet more efficiently affected the children's and parent's weight, blood sugar level, and blood cholesterol levels.

· JAMA Intern Med.2019: Diet and Risk of type 2 diabetes and plant-based diets: This original investigation was done in 2019 to know about the association of plant-based dietary patterns and the risk of type 2 diabetes. This meta-analysis was done by Harvard T.H Chan School of public health that people having more association with plant-based diets had a 23% lower risk of type 2 diabetes than ones who consumed less whole plant foods.
This data gives large evidence as was done including 307,099 people with almost 23,544 cases of 2 type diabetes. The association was stronger for people following healthy plant-based diets.
The systematic review explained the mechanism of association between reduced risk of diabetes 2 and diets of plant-based origin. According to researchers, plant diets improve blood pressure and sensitivity of insulin, reduce chances of weight gain, and suppress systemic inflammation. All of these factors, if not controlled, contribute to the risk of type 2 diabetes.

· National library of medicine article (2018); Hospital-based study on a vegan diet and high blood pressure:
A vegan diet is investigated to lower blood pressure and this was done to know about the effect of a vegan diet on blood pressure in participants who are asymptomatic with proteinuria is unknown. The examination was done to check the association between a vegan diet and blood pressure in participants with proteinuria and without

proteinuria.

This analysis was done from Sep 5, 2005, to Dec 21, 2016, in Taipei Tzu Chi hospital. Participants were more than 40 years old who used to have physical checkups at the hospital. Results showed that the vegan diet followers on average had lower systolic pressure and lower diastolic pressure than those who consumed omnivorous diets. Participants with proteinuria had higher systolic pressure and diastolic pressure than those with no proteinuria. The analysis further explained that vegans with proteinuria had low systolic and diastolic blood pressure than omnivorous eaters with proteinuria. Conclusions derived stated clearly that vegan diets are linked to lower blood pressure.

SUMMARY

The Vegan revolution is on its way! Veganism is abstaining from all animal products from life once and for all and adopting a lifestyle of true nature by eating plant-derived food. I hope this book has given you a complete informative guide about veganism, its roots from ancient times, and how it evolved from different religions, cultures, and traditions. The important sections are about nutritional value, vegan transitions, vegan evolution, and everything that you must know before going on a vegan diet. The perplexed notion about veganism and vegetarianism is emphasized to make it clear that they might seem similar but deep-down the realities for both concepts differ a lot. Veganism is a simple answer to the complex questions of disease prevention and reversal of many disorders. People go vegan for different environmental, political, religious, and health reasons. However, out of all, the health benefits of a vegan diet are attracting the public the most, as going vegan does wonders for your health.

According to multiple researches conducted, it is shown that almost a hundred years from now the whole population on earth is going to be vegan. Because of the current practices where animals are slaughtered to feed the people and the environment at its prime is hurting constantly, this can't go on forever and sooner or later an alternative has to be found and adapted and the vegan diet can just be that alternative solution the world needs. By going vegan, you are not only helping your body and freeing your soul but you are also favoring the continuity of Mother Nature so it can cherish human life for many years to come. With climate change and mass destruction of animal and forest life, it is not possible at all. A sudden transition from all such ill practices in the form of adapting the vegan diet culture is probably just what we need right now.

Another chapter delves into explaining how a vegan diet aids you in losing weight, becoming fit, and increasing lifespan. One can be a healthy and delighted vegan without cracking the whole vegan cookbook. Saying that only whole grain items work for a healthy vegan diet is a myth. Several delicious and nutritious vegan meal plans for beginners and strict vegans are given including varying plant food groups to devour your taste buds. Vegan fasting is a trending practice nowadays as it is an effective tool to combat obesity and chronic diseases, improve longevity, endurance, and mood.

However, proper guidance mentioned in the section about different protocols and intake of necessary eatables during fasting cycles must be considered. Dining out at restaurants and following vegan restrictions is not impossible, but one must know the tips and tricks to hack out every restaurant.

If you are a healthy vegan, enjoying the perks of being vegan, then you should also be a Vegan Ambassador. Contribute to the vegan movement by convincing others to try vegan diets; select a compassionate mindset, and show them practical results. Mountains of research-based evidence and scientific studies are there to support veganism. Veganism is not self-immolation. It is self-improvement and self-satisfaction.

REFERENCES

https://familydoctor.org/vegan-diet-how-to-get-the-nutrients-you-need/ https://familydoctor.org/vegan-diet-how-to-get-the-nutrients-you-need/

https://www.myfooddata.com/articles/zinc-foods-for-vegans-vegetarians.php https://www.healthline.com/nutrition/7-supplements-for-vegans#5.-Iron

https://www.quora.com/Does-the-taurine-deficiency-in-veg-ans-have anynegative-health-effects

https://www.nhs.uk/live-well/eat-well/vegetarian-and-vegan-diets-q-and-a/

https://spoonuniversity.com/healthier/21-things-i-learned-af- ter-going-vegan-for-21-days https://www.thehealthy.com/nutrition/vitamin-deficiency-vegetarian-vegan/

https://veganhealth.org/daily-needs/ https://www.theplantway.com/plant-sources-iodine/ https://www.vegansociety.com/resources/nutri-tion-and-health/nutrients/iodine

https://oldwayspt.org/blog/vitamin-d-sources-vegans-and-vegetarians https://gentleworld.org/optimizing-your-vegan-diet/

http://www.vegan-supplement-checklist.com/2008/10/tau-rine-and-l-glutamine.html

https://www.rian_Diet_and_Athletes

https://pubmed.ncbi.nlm.nih.gov/30069127/

https://inourishgently.com/16-scientific-studies-veganism/

https://www.healthline.com/nutrition/vegan-diet-studies

https://www.peta.org.uk/blog/7-ways-to-persuade-others-to-go-vegan/

https://madrabbits.org/2015/10/05/convincing-someone-to-go-vegan-in-one-paragraph/

https://www.vegansociety.com/news/blog/4-great-tips-help-your-friends-go-vegan

https://veganbeautyreview.com/2020/09/4-ways-convince-family-vegan.html: https://www.quora.com/How-would-you-convince-me-to-be- come-a-vegan

https://outwittrade.com/how-to-convince-people-to-go-vegan/

https://www.youtube.com/watch?v=E7LuZW5B4AU [: https://www.vegan.io/blog/how-to-eat-vegan-at-any-restaurant.html

https://ohsheglows.com/2013/02/06/10-tips-for-eating-out-as-a-vegan/

https://chooseveg.com/blog/here-are-14-delicious-vegan-options-at-your/ [https://www.peta.org/living/food/chain-restaurants/

https://www.researchgate.net/publication/319696943_Vegan_diets_Practical_advice_for_athletes_and_exercisers

http://www.organicathlete.org/pub/OAGuide_pdf.pdf

https://www.weightlossresources.co.uk/nutrition/vitamins/vitamin_a.htm

https://trace.tennessee.edu/cgi/viewcontent.cgi?article=4939&-context=utk_gradthes

https://www.webmd.com/a-to-z-guides/supplement-guide-vitamin-a#1

Printed in Great Britain
by Amazon